P9-CQN-059

Music Was IT

Young Leonard Bernstein

Music Was IT

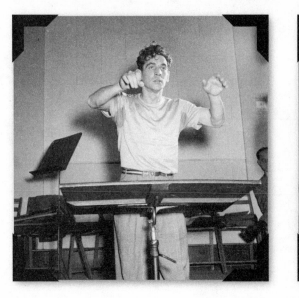

Young Leonard Bernstein

SUSAN GOLDMAN RUBIN

Charlesbridge

Captions for photographs used in the front matter:
Cover collage: Lenny conducting in rehearsal at Carnegie Hall; Lenny conducting the Camp
Onota Rhythm Band, 1937; Lenny conducting Stravinsky's *L'Historie de Soldat* at an informal tea
party, Tanglewood, August 1940; a page of the score for "I Hate Music!" handwritten by Lenny.
p. i: Lenny at about three years old.
pp. ii–iii: Lenny conducting in rehearsal at Carnegie Hall.
p. vi: Lenny conducting the New York City Symphony, 1945.
p. viii: Lenny's graduation photo from Boston Latin School, 1935. The inscription is to
Helen Coates, his piano teacher and later his secretary.
p. xi: Lenny with daughter Jamie, 1957.
p. xii: Lenny playing piano at a Tanglewood party.

First paperback edition 2015
Copyright © 2011 by Susan Goldman Rubin
All rights reserved, including the right of reproduction in whole or in part in any form.
Charlesbridge and colophon are registered trademarks of Charlesbridge Publishing, Inc.

The sources of quotations beginning on page 157 and the credits beginning on page 169
comprise an extension of this copyright page. We have made every effort to locate and
obtain permission from the rights holders of images and quotations used in this book.
Please contact the publisher if you have further information on rights holders.

Published by Charlesbridge
85 Main Street
Watertown, MA 02472
(617) 926-0329
www.charlesbridge.com

Library of Congress Cataloging-in-Publication Data
Rubin, Susan Goldman.
  Music was it : young Leonard Bernstein / Susan Goldman Rubin.
    p. cm.
  ISBN 978-1-58089-344-2 (reinforced hardcover)
  ISBN 978-1-58089-345-9 (softcover)
  ISBN 978-1-60734-773-6 (ebook)
  ISBN 978-1-60734-276-2 (ebook pdf)
1. Bernstein, Leonard, 1918–1990—Juvenile literature. 2. Musicians—
United States—Biography—Juvenile literature. I. Title.
ML3930.B48R83 2011
780.92—dc22 [B]   2010007584

Printed in the United States of America
(hc) 10 9 8 7 6 5 4 3 2
(sc) 10 9 8 7 6 5 4 3 2 1

Display type set in Cyclone by Swfte International, and Felt Tip Roman by Mark Simonson
Text type set in Goudy Old Style by Type Solutions, Inc.
Color separations by Chroma Graphics, Singapore
Printed by Worzalla Publishing Company in Stevens Point, Wisconsin, USA
Production supervision by Brian G. Walker
Designed by Diane M. Earley

To John B. Goldman and Andrew A. Rubin,
and in memory of Edward Kleban (1939–1987)
—S. G. R.

Table of Contents

Foreword ix

1. Moynik 1

2. In Love with a Piano 9

3. Crazed and Raging Fingers 21

4. Lenny the Showman 33

5. Lenny at Harvard 45

6. Genius Boy 53

7. Crazy Artist Nuts 57

8. November 14th 63

9. Glimmering Possibility 73

10. Me? A Conductor? 77

11. Work and Work and Work 85

12. What to Do Next? 103

13. On the Town 115

14. Suddenly Famous 125

Epilogue 135

Timeline 138

Biographies 140

Lenny's Music (includes Discography and Bibliography) 151

Sources of Quotations 157

Photo Credits and Permissions 169

Acknowledgments 172

Index 175

To Helen Coates,
a fine teacher
and great friend
Leonard Bernstein

Foreword

Every time I revisit my father's personal story, I'm swept up again by its dramatic arc, its iconic theme of artistic expression triumphing over parental disapproval, and the sheer blind luck of it all.

As a little girl growing up in our happy, noisy family, I didn't really understand why my father was such a big deal. Sure, he was a great musician, and he was pretty handsome—and most impressive of all, he was on TV! But seriously: what was all the fuss about? Only as an adult did I begin to comprehend the impact Leonard Bernstein had on his American contemporaries at that particular time in history.

On the afternoon of November 14, 1943, as that skinny, trembling 25-year-old hopped onto the podium in Carnegie Hall, the United States was barely pulling out of the Great Depression and now found itself in the clutches of a ghastly World War. It was a frightening time in America; people needed some good news. American Jews needed good news even more desperately, as reports trickled back over the ocean from Treblinka, Warsaw, Bergen-Belsen. No wonder the newspapers leaped on Leonard Bernstein's debut the next day, exuberantly telling his story on their front pages. It was, in fact, pretty big news that an American-born, American-trained, young Jewish man from Massachusetts had ascended that reserved-for-Europeans podium at all— and then proceeded to knock the music right out of the park.

Overnight success! Just like in the movies, except it really happened. It had not been a cinch for Leonard Bernstein to get there. Maybe the toughest part for him was the constant disapproval and lack of support from his father, Sam. The more fiercely young Lenny felt the need to be a musician, the more strongly Sam Bernstein discouraged him. (To be fair, Sam was protectively worried that a musician in America would be little more than a beggar, which was the condition of musicians back in the Russian villages of Sam's childhood.)

Some would say that a parent's disapproval will actually focus a young artist's drive and make it stronger. Whether or not that's true, there's no arguing that a parent withholding approval will make any child's life a tougher, colder place. This sad environment may also have given my father the resolve to be as supportive as possible to his own children. I don't think my brother, sister, or I ever felt less than joyously welcome in our father's presence. He was curious and appreciative about all our interests: from the Flintstones to the Yankees to the Beatles. (OK, maybe not so much Barbie.)

On that November afternoon at Carnegie Hall, there was no way for Leonard Bernstein to know what was in store for him: the global conducting triumphs, the Broadway scores, the TV shows, the wife, the kids. All he knew that day was that he'd gotten an incredibly lucky break when Maestro Bruno Walter fell ill, and he knew he had to make the most of it. It was a perfect coincidence of talent, timing and opportunity. Such coincidences are an eternal source of fascination to us. On the other hand, maybe, as my father was fond of saying, "There are no coincidences."

—Jamie Bernstein

"Life without music is unthinkable."

—Leonard Bernstein, *Findings*

Lenny at age two.

1

Moynik

From the start Leonard loved music. When he was about two years old, his parents, Sam and Jennie, stayed with friends who had a summer house at Revere Beach near Boston. The friends had a piano in the living room, and whenever Leonard heard someone playing, he pressed his ear to the closed door. "Moynik!" he shouted, his own word for music.

At home in Mattapan, a suburb of Boston, he would cry "Moynik!" with tears running down his face until his mother put a record on the windup Victrola. Then Lenny, as he was called, would stop crying and listen happily. The Victrola was Lenny's faithful companion and, often, his only playmate.

Lenny at age four with his parents, Jennie and Samuel.

Lenny was a sickly boy with asthma. "Every time he had an attack," said his mother, "we thought he was going to die." She stayed up all night "with steam kettles and hot towels, helping him to breathe." If he so much as sneezed or seemed to be coming down with a cold, she kept him indoors. At ages four and five, Lenny amused himself by sitting at the window of the front room and watching people pass by as he listened to the Victrola. One of his favorite tunes was a popular song called "Oh by Jingo": "Oh by jingo! Oh by gee!/ You're the only girl for me." He also enjoyed recordings of opera singers and Jewish cantors. From his perch indoors, he would tap rhythmically on the windowsill in time to the music, so his mother called him her "windowsill pianist."

In 1923, when he was five, his sister was born. Their mother named her Shirley Anne, after Anne Shirley, the heroine of her favorite book, *Anne of Green Gables*, and the actress Anne Shirley, who later starred in the movie version. For the first few years until the family rented a larger apartment, Lenny and Shirley shared a room. She became his closest ally, and they thought of themselves as a separate family.

During Lenny's childhood his greatest musical influence came from the synagogue. Because his father was a deeply religious man, the family joined Temple Mishkan Tefila and went to services on Friday nights, the big music night. Mishkan Tefila was a conservative congregation that allowed an organ and a mixed choir of men and women. The music moved Lenny deeply and brought tears to his eyes. The

Young Lenny and Shirley.

cantor sang "the ancient tunes," Lenny remembered. "Then the organ would start and then the choir would begin with its colors, and I just began to get crazed with the sound of choral music." The organist and choirmaster was Professor Solomon Braslavsky, a musician trained in Vienna. Braslavsky was also a composer and performed many of his own compositions during services. Once he created an arrangement of the hymn "Adon Olam" ("Lord of the World") for High Holy Days. "Arrangement is too small a word," said Lenny. "It was a great composition. I knew every note of it because I heard it every year; it was like an opera." Later as an adult, Lenny said that Braslavsky provided him

4

with "the first real music I heard." In a letter to Braslavsky he wrote, "I never forget the tremendous influence you and your music made on me when I was a youngster."

For a long time Lenny thought of becoming a rabbi. His ancestors on his father's side were scholarly rabbis. Sam's Judaism pervaded the household. Born in the town of Beresdiv in the Russian Ukraine and raised as a Hasidic Orthodox Jew, Sam had lived in a *shtetl*, a Jewish village. At age sixteen he had come to America against his parents' wishes. Sam struggled to make a good living. First he cleaned fish in a market in New York City, then he worked at his uncle's barbershop in

Solomon Braslavsky (with outstretched arm) with Jewish musicians in Europe.

Connecticut. Finally he wound up selling barber and beauty supplies for a company in Boston.

In 1923 Sam opened his own business, the Samuel Bernstein Hair Company. Mostly he made and sold wigs to Orthodox Jewish women, who were traditionally required to keep their own hair covered. In 1927 his business grew when he bought a license to sell a new invention—the Frederics Permanent Wave machine for curling women's hair. His was the only company in New England that sold the machine, and beauty parlors swamped him with orders. "It was what you call the American Dream coming true," said Sam.

Miss America receives a permanent wave with the newfangled permanent wave machine in 1926.

Lenny's mother, Jennie, was also Jewish and had emigrated from the Old Country when she was six years old. As a little girl in Russia, she liked to wander through non-Jewish parts of town, listening to strolling street musicians. Once she followed the musicians and got lost. She fell asleep in a park, and the next morning a czarist policeman dragged her home. As a teenager in America,

Lenny with his parents, Samuel and Jennie, and his sister, Shirley, around 1933.

Jennie was forced to drop out of school and work in the Massachusetts textile mills to help support her family. Then she married and started raising her own children.

Like many other Jewish immigrant families, the Bernsteins moved frequently to bigger apartments in better areas as Sam's income increased. By the time Lenny was nine, they were living in Roxbury. On the way home from school, bigger boys chased him. Frail and skinny, Lenny didn't know how to fight back.

Then when he was ten, a miracle happened. Almost overnight his health improved, he shot up in height to be the tallest boy on the block, and he could run faster than anyone else.

All because of a piano.

2

In Love with a Piano

Lenny's family had never owned a piano. But when his aunt Clara, his father's sister, moved from Massachusetts to New York, she gave them her sofa and her rickety old upright piano. Lenny's parents appreciated having the sofa and made room for it right away. But they didn't want the piano or know where to put it, so they kept it in the hallway. For Lenny, however, it was love at first sight. "I remember touching this thing the day it arrived," he later recalled, "just stroking it and going mad. I knew, from that moment to this, that music was 'it.' There was no question in my mind that my life was to be about music."

At that time Lenny attended the William Lloyd Garrison School in Roxbury. He was a good student and enjoyed learning everything, from history and spelling to "fun things [such] as drawing." What he loved best of all, however, were the "singing hours."

"Mrs. Fitzgerald, my fifth-grade homeroom teacher, taught us many dozens of songs," he later recalled. Lenny was a terrible singer, with a high squeaky voice, but he joined in enthusiastically. Any form of music thrilled him—but the piano at home obsessed him. "I was safe at the piano," he remembered. "I suddenly felt at the center of a universe I could control. . . . This thing [the piano] suddenly made me feel supreme." How could he learn how to play? He started by picking out songs he had heard on the radio. The first was a new favorite, "Good Night, Sweetheart."

"I knew it had to have a fox-trot accompaniment," said Lenny. "But I didn't know what notes to play in the left hand so I would just play anything . . . loudly and triumphantly."

Shirley liked going to sleep every night to the sound of Lenny's playing. For her, "Good Night, Sweetheart" was a lullaby—but not for Sam.

As Lenny hammered out the notes, his father would yell from the bedroom, "Stop that noise, I can't sleep!"

"But I," said Lenny, "was in heaven."

Lenny "demanded piano lessons," which he got "because nobody took it seriously and nobody thought I was really going to be a musician," he recalled. "Only I knew that." The Bernsteins' neighbors, the Karps, had two daughters who taught piano. Frieda Karp was selected as Lenny's teacher and came to the apartment once a week to give him lessons. "After a couple of weeks," said Lenny, "I had learned to read [music] so quickly—I was very fast—that Frieda Karp had to bring me harder stuff."

Lenny started with a piece for beginners called "Mountain Belle Schottische." Next Frieda brought him a green-covered book called *100 Pieces the Whole World Loves* that included works by Bach and Chopin. When he played the Chopin E-flat Nocturne, his mother stood there crying.

"This boy is gifted," Frieda told Lenny's mother after she had been teaching him for two years. "I can't keep up with him anymore." She recommended that Lenny find another teacher at the New England Conservatory of Music in Boston. "On my own," wrote Lenny, "I went to the New England Conservatory of Music—that's where you learn to be a good pianist, somebody had told me—and I was assigned to a Miss Susan Williams. She charged three dollars an hour, and all hell broke loose between Sam and me. He saw that things were getting serious, and he was not going to spend three dollars a lesson. So the fights began."

Sam said, "You get one dollar a week for piano lessons and that is it."

What really worried Sam was Lenny's "scary dedication" to piano studies. Music as a hobby on the weekend was fine, but not as a full-time career. Like many successful men in those days, Sam dreamed of having his son go into business with him and eventually take over. By this time Sam's company had grown, and he had a staff of fifty

NEW ENGLAND CONSERVATORY OF MUSIC

RECITAL HALL

WEDNESDAY EVENING, MARCH 30, 1932, AT 8:15 O'CLOCK

PIANOFORTE RECITAL

by

Pupils of Susan Williams

❦ ❦

PROGRAM

MENDELSSOHN . . . Spring Song
STOJOWSKI . . . . . Danse Humoresque
          KATHERINE MAGILL

GHYS . . . . Amaryllis (Air by King Louis XIII.)
          BEATRICE DROOKER

PADEREWSKI . . . Minuet in G
          HARRIET SCHLESINGER

TCHAIKOVSKY . . . June
SCHUBERT . . . . . Scherzo in B♭
          ALICE SMITH

MENDELSSOHN . . Venetian Gondola Song in F♯ minor
          CARL PIERNI

BEETHOVEN . . . . Contra Dance in C major
GRIEG . . . . . . Grandmother's Minuet
DURAND . . . . . Valse in E♭
          DOROTHY GOLDSTEIN

GRIEG . . . . . . Butterfly
PALMGREN . . . . May Night
          MARY CLARE WRIGHT

RACHMANINOV . . Prelude in G♯ minor
          LORETTA METZGER

D. SCARLATTI . . Sonata in D minor
MOZART . . . . . Andante from Sonata in G major
BACH . . . . . . Two-Part Invention in B♭
          BARBARA MAYOR

CYRIL SCOTT . . . Lento
SCHUMANN . . . . Romance in F♯ major
DEBUSSY . . . . . Clair de lune
          PHYLLIS BELMORE

PADEREWSKI . . . Cracovienne fantastique
SCHUETT . . . . . Tendre aveu
BRAHMS . . . . . Rhapsody in G minor
          LEONARD BERNSTEIN

Steinway Pianoforte

Program, Pupils of Miss Susan Williams, March 30, 1932.

employees. A small fleet of trucks emblazoned with the words *In Boston It's Bernstein* drove through town, delivering beauty supplies. Beauty parlors and permanent waves had become a craze, and Sam was making a great deal of money. He had worked hard to achieve financial success and security, and he wanted to pass it on to his son. The only exception would be if Lenny had a religious calling and became a rabbi. "Under no circumstances," Sam said, "would Lenny be a musician." To Sam a musician was a *klezmer*. In Russia a *klezmer* was a poor musician, usually a fiddler or clarinetist, who roamed from town to town, playing at weddings and bar mitzvahs for very little money and perhaps some food. The American equivalent was a pianist who played in cocktail lounges or a dance band. "American Jewish boys had no chance in the field of serious music," said Sam.

And he was right. At that time—1930—great pianists, violinists, and opera singers were European-born and trained, and they performed in America with orchestras conducted by other Europeans.

Lenny's mother, however, encouraged his music. "Lenny always played at night," Jennie said. "Of course it disturbed his father's sleep. But I would listen way into the night." In Russia she had followed the *klezmer* musicians around town and had enjoyed their music. Now she loved the sound of her son playing the piano in her own house. Sometimes, when she thought no one was listening, she went to the piano herself and played the one piece she knew by heart, "Dolly's Waltz."

Lenny finally solved the problem of paying for his lessons by saving almost all of his allowance. He earned the rest by giving piano lessons himself to little kids and charging a dollar an hour. His first student was Sid Ramin, another twelve-year-old boy in the neighborhood. They met one day at the house of a mutual friend, Eddie Ryack. Lenny was trying to teach Eddie how to play "Good Night, Sweetheart" on the piano. Eddie was having trouble. Sid had been listening to Lenny's unique instructions and said, "Mind if I try?" He sat down at the piano and played the piece perfectly.

"You're the fellow I should be teaching," said Lenny. And from then on, he did.

"We would sit down at the piano, and he would show me stuff," remembered Sid. When they went to the movies together, they hurried back to Lenny's house and tried to play four-hand arrangements of some of the music they had heard. The boys forged a friendship based on music that lasted all their lives. "We were inseparable," recalled Sid.

Under Lenny's guidance Sid quickly became a good pianist, and the two boys played four-hand duets. When they first heard George Gershwin's *Rhapsody in Blue*, they were crazy about it. "We bought the sheet music of the piano solo arrangement," said Lenny, "and we went home and played it with tears till dawn."

"I was there when his father gave him the money to buy the score," said Sid. "He had to beg for the two dollars. We went back to Lenny's place, and at sight he began to play it. Incredible. He was a prodigious sight reader."

Sid was also admitted to a secret society Lenny had formed with Eddie two years earlier, when they were both ten. Inspired by studying

Sid "Syd" Ramin, 1936.

ancient history at grammar school, the boys had created their own country called Rybernia. The name was a combination of their two last names, Ryack and Bernstein. They even thought up their own funny language, Rybernian, based largely on the Yiddish accent of Lenny's father. Most likely it was Lenny who composed a national anthem sung to the tune of a hit song, "When the Moon Comes Over the Mountain." Shirley, at age five, was the club's mascot.

When Lenny and Shirley's baby brother was born in January 1932, he was admitted as a member. At that time Lenny was in the middle of his first year at the prestigious Boston Latin School. That very week he had been studying alliteration in poetry and liked the sound of two words starting with the same consonant. So Lenny named the baby Burton, because it went well with Bernstein. His parents agreed because Burton started with a B, and they wanted to name the baby in honor of his paternal great-grandfather, Bezalel, according to Jewish tradition. From then on Lenny and Shirley thought of themselves as a private Rybernian family at home. They were the parents, and they pretended that their little brother, nicknamed Burtie, was their child. Their "closed society," with its own humor, language, and private jokes, lasted into their adulthood. As children, though, they huddled together for comfort when they heard their mother and father fighting.

Sam and Jennie were not happily married. Like many couples in those days, they stayed together despite their differences. Later Shirley said that her parents were both fine people, but not a good match.

Burtie and Sam, 1935.

Sometimes Sam and Jennie argued about money. Sam could be generous on occasion but at other times tightfisted. "The more money he had," Burton wrote later, "the more he feared losing it."

Often the fights centered on Lenny's music. Jennie approved; Sam did not. He would say to Lenny, "You know, you can play the piano all

17

Sam and Lenny on vacation on Mt. Monadnock, New Hampshire.

you want. It's a wonderful thing to come home at night and relax at the piano after a hard day. But if you're going to be a *mensch* [a successful, honorable person] and support a family, you can't be a *klezmer*."

"His father was nagging him all the time about making a living," remembered Lenny's friend Sid. "He [Sam] was very practical. Very stern. He wanted his son to be a success."

18

Success to Sam meant working for the Bernstein Hair Company or becoming a rabbi. Sam valued education, and he was proud of Lenny for doing so well at Boston Latin and at Hebrew school, where he studied every day after regular school and from which he eventually graduated with honors. At age thirteen, when Lenny had his bar mitzvah, he gave two speeches, one in Hebrew and one in English, before hundreds of members of Temple Mishkan Tefila. Most boys took their choice of six or seven "prefabricated" speeches, but Lenny wrote his own. Sam, who was vice president of the congregation, sat up on the *bimah*, beaming. He rewarded Lenny with a gift of a Chickering grand piano to replace Aunt Clara's old upright. Sam may also have purchased the piano as a status symbol to show off his prosperity. At that

Graduation picture from Congregation Mishkan Tefila's Hebrew school, 1931. Lenny is in the second row, fourth from right.

time many Jewish families, even poor ones, bought pianos (sometimes on the installment plan) as a sign of "making it" in America.

It was Sam who took Lenny at age fourteen to his first public concert at Symphony Hall. He said to Lenny, "I have two tickets for a benefit for the temple tonight, and I don't know what to do with them. Maybe you would like to go."

Lenny said, "Would I like to go?"

They went and heard the Boston Pops, conducted by Arthur Fiedler, perform Ravel's *Bolero*. Lenny was ecstatic. "I remember . . . being so thrilled with [*Bolero*] at that concert that I saved up for two or three months so I could buy a piano arrangement," he said.

Even Sam loved the music, because it reminded him of Hebrew chants. "He thought it was the most wonderful thing he had ever heard," said Lenny. "That shed a ray of light . . . because I was in a state of rebellion against him."

What's more, Fiedler was Jewish and lived in Brookline, a suburb of Boston. There was hope. Could a Jew from Boston really make it as a musician?

3

Crazed and Raging Fingers

Bolero brought Lenny and his father closer together—at least for a while. It was now Sam's favorite piece and gave him a new interest in classical music. Yet he still insisted that music was not an acceptable career. Lenny recalled that his father kept saying to him, "'Why don't you become a rabbi if you won't go into my business?' He was convinced that I would never be able to support myself or a family as a musician."

Nevertheless, Sam loved Lenny and wanted to do something special for his older son. Sam bought tickets for another concert at Symphony Hall for the two of them. This time they heard a recital by Sergey Rachmaninoff, a Russian pianist and composer. "It was a very severe program with a . . . late Beethoven sonata," recalled Lenny. "Sam didn't understand it at all, but he suffered through it. I was thrilled to pieces."

Lenny gave one of his first public performances at the family's synagogue, Temple Mishkan Tefila. He was only fourteen, but Sam invited him to play for a Brotherhood dinner, an event sponsored by the temple's men's club. "I don't think people listened very hard that night to what I played on the piano," Lenny recalled. "For one thing, they had all just eaten a big, heavy, kosher meal; and besides, what I played probably wasn't very good." The piece Lenny played was his own composition. Later he described it as "variations on a tune my father was very fond of singing in the shower, and from hearing it sung so often I had gotten to be rather fond of it myself." The tune was a Hasidic song. Lenny performed the theme in the different styles of great composers: Bach, Chopin, and Gershwin. Sam was delighted and very proud, especially when members of the Brotherhood congratulated him.

That winter Sam took Lenny for a cruise to Miami, just the two of them. Although the Great Depression had crippled the country's economy and had thrown many people into poverty, the Bernstein family's finances were secure. Sam had owned no stock, so he was unaffected by the stock market crash; he had saved his money instead of investing it in the market. Furthermore, his business was booming. Despite the skimpy budgets of most Americans, many women spent a little something at the beauty shop to have a permanent wave. So Sam was able to afford the cruise. "The first night, after dinner," he recalled, "Lenny and I took a walk through the ship. He spotted a beautiful big piano. It was about seven thirty. Most of the passengers were still at dinner. Lenny sat down at the piano. In about an hour, the whole

Lenny in Florida, December 1933. He wrote a postcard to Miss Coates that began, "This place is beyond description. . . . I have created quite a stir with the piano."

salon was filled. At midnight he was still playing." As part of his entertainment, Lenny played the same variations on his father's tune that he had performed at the synagogue. People in the audience gave him requests for other composers, and he improvised on the spot.

Lenny passed on his love of music to his sister, Shirley. At home he played duets with her and taught her how to sight-read quickly.

"How?" she said. "He hit me if I did it wrong. He also taught me how to get through a piece, how to fake it, how to play the harmonies with the left hand while keeping the melody going with the right." Shirley had started taking piano lessons when she was nine, on Aunt Clara's old piano. But she knew that she didn't play nearly as well as her brother. Shirley could hear him practicing upstairs on the new grand piano, his bar mitzvah gift. "The competition was getting impossible," she recalled. "It was very hard for me to practice my scales and my simple little pieces when I heard Lenny pounding away at the Grieg concerto and other hard pieces." So when Shirley asked her mother if she could stop taking formal lessons, Jennie readily agreed. "There's enough noise in this house already," said Jennie. But Shirley's love of music went on and flourished with Lenny as her teacher.

When Shirley was about ten and Lenny was fourteen or fifteen, he took scores out of the public library for them to play together as four-hand duets. They started with symphonies and tone poems, then progressed to operas. "It was terribly exciting," said Shirley. "We were creating music. We played four-hand symphonies and I sang my lungs out." When they did operas such as Bizet's *Carmen* and Verdi's *Aida*, "he'd be all the guys, I'd be all the girls," said Shirley, "and we'd both be all the chorus. . . . Oh, it was fun." Since neither of them had ever been to the opera before, they didn't know how it was supposed to sound. "We just sailed into it," said Shirley, "all flags flying." They played "into the wee hours of the night."

At two o'clock in the morning, Sam would appear at the top of the stairs and bellow, "Stop that damn piano! You make so much noise, and I got a big day at the office tomorrow." But they kept playing anyway, as if, said Jennie, they were "chained to the piano."

Lenny's friends recalled that he would walk into somebody's house and head straight for the piano, forgetting to take off his coat. And he would stand rather than sit as he played. Lenny remembered that he "stayed there until they threw me out. It was as though I didn't exist without music." One of his close friends, Mildred Spiegel, said that when he came to her house he would sit down at the piano, a new Baldwin grand, "and play any music that happened to be there, sight-reading as fast as if he'd been playing it for years." He played so hard that he often broke a string, which the tuner had to replace.

Lenny had met Mildred in the fall of 1932, when he was fourteen and she was sixteen. One day after finishing classes at Boston Latin, he came over to her school, Roxbury Memorial High School for Girls. "I found him playing *Malaguena* by Lecuona on the Steinway grand in a long, empty auditorium surrounded by a small group of admiring students," she remembered. "I was astonished at his sense of drama, stupendous enthusiasm. . . . His playing sounded like an orchestra."

Madison Trio. From left to right: Mildred Spiegel, Sarah Kruskall, and Dorothy Rosenberg.

From then on Lenny and Mildred became "musical friends." Every Tuesday afternoon they played duets and piano pieces together, sometimes meeting at the New England Conservatory, where they both took lessons. Mildred thought Lenny was a genius and "would one day be famous."

"Do you really think so?" he asked.

26

"After rehearsals," she recalled, "he bought a five-cent chocolate Nestlé bar and a two-cent portion of *halvah* [a Turkish candy made of sesame seeds and honey], which he loved." And they talked. Lenny told Mildred that his father "resented" his seriousness about a musical career and they "had a constant conflict." But she encouraged Lenny and gave him support. In the fall of 1933, they bought a subscription for Saturday night concerts of the Boston Symphony Orchestra and sat in the cheapest seats, high up in the second balcony. One evening, after hearing Serge Koussevitzky conduct, the audience stood and gave the conductor a standing ovation. Lenny just sat there. Mildred said to him, "What's the matter? Didn't you like it?"

"Not like it?" said Lenny. "I loved it! That's the trouble. I'm just jealous of any man who can make music like that."

At that point Lenny had no thoughts of becoming a conductor. To him conductors were exclusively European, like Koussevitzky from Russia and Arturo Toscanini from Italy. Only Fiedler was American—and even he had studied in Berlin. Lenny's focus was the piano.

He and Mildred became popular at parties, where they entertained everyone. Sometimes she sang and he accompanied her, or they played a duet, such as their favorite, *Rumbalero* by Morton Gould. It was written for two pianos, but they played it on one.

Through his friendship with Mildred, Lenny realized that he was not getting proper training as a pianist. His teacher, Miss Williams, had taught him to not arch his hands over the keyboard the way most pianists did. Instead she wanted him to keep his fingers a certain way:

"bent over the keys but with no third knuckles showing." It was torture for Lenny—and it was incorrect. When he asked Mildred to play solos for him, he admired her technique. Mildred was studying with the best teacher in Boston, Heinrich Gebhard. She suggested that Lenny audition for him, and he did.

Gebhard said that Lenny needed to work on technique and suggested that he study with his best assistant, Miss Helen Coates. She charged six dollars an hour. Gebhard agreed to give Lenny a lesson from time to time for fifteen dollars an hour. "When Sam heard of this new arrangement," wrote Lenny, "he screamed bloody murder. There would come these terrible diatribes about the *klezmer* again, that the *klezmer* was no better than a beggar."

So Lenny earned the money for lessons himself by playing at weddings and bar mitzvahs (just like a *klezmer*) with a small jazz group he had formed with friends. When he had earned enough, Lenny politely wrote to Miss Coates, "Having talked the matter over at home, I have decided to study with you, taking one lesson every two weeks."

Miss Coates was a young woman, not much older than Lenny. Right away she recognized his talent. Before long she scheduled his lesson for the end of the day, so that she could extend a one-hour lesson to three hours. During the second hour Lenny played opera scores, which fascinated him. They sat side by side at two keyboards, and she corrected the way he held his hands. Lenny said, "She taught me how not to 'bang,' how to use the pedal discreetly, how to discipline my crazed and raging fingers."

Miss Helen Coates in her studio. The inscription reads, "To my dearest pupil, Leonard Bernstein, in recent remembrances of your great success on May 14th and of many joyful hours of study—from your teacher and friend, Helen Coates, Boston, 1934."

Sat. at 1:00 Oct. 22

8 Pleasanton St.,
Roxbury, Mass.
Oct. 15, 1932

Dear Miss Coates:

I recently had an inter-
view with Mr. Gebhard at
his home. He was very en-
couraging in his remarks, and
referred me to you as a teacher,
with an occasional lesson from
himself.

Having talked the mat-
ter over at home, I have decided to study with you, taking
one lesson every two weeks.

Lenny's letter to Miss Coates, October 15, 1932

2.

Would you please let me know by mail or 'phone when it would be convenient for you to give me my first lesson?

Hoping to have the pleasure of studying with you soon,

Sincerely Yours,

Leonard Bernstein.

P.S. If you should decide to call me, my 'phone number is Garrison 8141.

L.B.

She said that he was the "quickest learner" she ever had. "He could read, sing, and memorize anything." Each year he was one of the top performers in her student recitals. Later Lenny said that she "gave me my first really important piano lessons."

At home, though, he still played loudly. The neighbors called and complained to Jennie. "Will you tell your son to stop banging on the piano? We can't sleep." And Jennie would say, "Someday you're going to pay to hear him!"

4

Lenny the Showman

During the summers of his teenage years, Lenny and his family stayed at their cottage in Sharon, a lakeside village. Sharon was one of the few country towns near Boston that was open to Jews in those days. The Bernsteins' Jewish neighborhood was called the Grove. Sam joined the local synagogue, Congregation Adath Sharon, so he could still worship when he was away from their synagogue in Boston. He also became its treasurer. On weekends the whole family and any guests who were visiting attended services, which were held in the rabbi's cottage.

Of course, Lenny could not give up music from June to September. So at the cottage he played on Aunt Clara's rickety old upright piano. The summer of 1933 he practiced the Grieg piano concerto in preparation for a recital the following spring. In a letter to his teacher,

Miss Coates, he wrote, "I can't seem to practice it enough. It is truly the most fascinating study I have ever entertained. . . . It is falling to my fingers surprisingly easily. I am confident that I shall have probably mastered it by the coming fall."

Lenny also played the score of *Bolero* that summer and drove his mother crazy. He wrote to his friend Sid Ramin, "I bought *Bolero*!!! So for the past week it's been nothing but *Bolero*. My mother says I'm boleroing her head off. But I am in heaven! It's all written in French and it's all repeats. . . . And the ending! Speaking of cacophony!! Boom! Crash! Discord!"

By the end of the summer, the piano was in bad shape, probably from Lenny's banging. "Now even the pedal fails to give results," he wrote to Miss Coates. "At the slightest hint of damp weather (of which we have had an unusual frequency this year at Sharon) the keys stick and are silent."

Back in Boston Lenny continued his piano lessons. In May 1934 he played the first movement of the Grieg piano concerto with the Boston Public School Orchestra. The orchestra was made up of the best student musicians from the local high schools. His friend Mildred Spiegel was the official pianist of the Boston Public School Senior Symphony, and the concert took place at her high school. She recalled that "many of the members were music majors and later joined the Boston Symphony Orchestra." The concert was Lenny's formal debut as a soloist. His mother attended the performance that evening, but his father did not.

Lenny was disappointed. Miss Coates understood how he felt and wrote to Sam, expressing her regret that he had not been there. Sam answered in a letter that he had been "unavoidably detained. While I am confident of his [Lenny's] progress in his musical education," he wrote, "I shall want him to continue to treasure his accomplishments in this connection solely from an idealistic viewpoint. . . . From a practical standpoint, I prefer that he does not regard his music as a future means of maintenance."

Lenny playing piano at age sixteen. Photo by Jennie Bernstein.

In other words, Sam still expected that Lenny would come to his senses and work in the Samuel Bernstein Hair Company.

Lenny had other ideas.

That summer in Sharon he continued his musical life with a new venture. He and his sister, Shirley, put on a show, a spoof of their favorite opera, *Carmen*. Using the battered upright piano, they eagerly went to work. Lenny's friend Dana Schnittken, a classmate from Boston Latin, helped produce the show. The boys wrote a short version of the opera "using just the hit tunes" and added inside jokes about Sharon. In Act I, for instance, the character Mercedes says, "Guess what? Don Jose [the male lead] is coming to Sharon. . . . He's coming to take part in the new contest. You know, Mr. Judah is giving away one big luscious hot dog to anyone who scores 8000 in his slot machine. And Don Jose just loves hot dogs." For fun they did the show in drag: the boys played girls' parts and the girls played boys' parts. Lenny said, "I sang Carmen in a red wig and a black mantilla and in a series of chiffon dresses borrowed from various neighbors on Lake Avenue [the street in Sharon where they lived], through which my underwear was showing." Don Jose was played by Beatrice Gordon, Lenny's new girlfriend, whom he described as "the love of my life." The wigs were supplied by the Samuel Bernstein Hair Company. Lenny wrote a prologue in verse explaining the story for his sister, Shirley (whose two front teeth were missing, which made her lisp), to recite at the beginning of the program. "Otherwise," said Lenny, "nobody would have gotten it." Lenny directed the show and choreographed the dances. He even made posters and printed the tickets.

The one and only perform-ance took place at Singer's Inn, the local hotel. "They had made the dining room available to us after dinner for this presenta-tion," recalled Lenny. "We hung up enormous white sheets to make a curtain and charged twenty-five cents." About two hundred peo-

Beatrice Gordon, around 1935.

ple attended. The kids collected around fifty dollars, which they gave to charity.

Lenny played the piano to accompany the singers. When he was "onstage" performing, his friend Mildred Spiegel took over for him. Lenny raced back and forth to the piano. "We were a smash," said Lenny. "Even Sam loved it. He lent us his wigs, after all. It was the sort of innocent musical fun he approved of for me—good relaxation but not a career."

But Lenny was beginning to discover his talent as a showman.

Back in Boston he completed his last year of high school. In an essay for his English class, he wrote about the conflict with his father. Respectfully he wrote that his father's business offered an "excellent means for development and improvement. On the other hand," he went on, "I care nothing for it, but am exceedingly interested in music.

Sam and Lenny at the beach, possibly in Sharon, around 1935.

In fact there is never a time when I do not prefer playing my piano to any other sort of work or recreation. It is true that because of rather than in spite of home discouragement [meaning Sam's disapproval], I am filled all the more with the desire for a musical life."

In June 1935 Lenny graduated from Boston Latin and co-wrote the class song. "It was a valedictory song for the graduating class to sing," recalled Lenny, and it "was the first completed work that I ever wrote down and drew a double bar [on]." (Drawing a double line in the last bar meant that the composition was ended.) Lenny composed the music and co-wrote the lyrics with a classmate, Lawrence F. Ebb. The song began,

> All for one and one for all.
> Sharing each success or fall;
> All too soon has come the parting
> To worldly realms beyond our wall.

That summer in Sharon, Lenny wanted to do another show. This time he chose *The Mikado* by Gilbert and Sullivan. Now Lenny, Shirley, and their friends called themselves the Sharon Players. Lenny directed and took the starring role of Nanki-Poo. Shirley played the part of Yum-Yum. And Lenny's friend Mildred joined them to play "the entire accompaniment" on the piano. Rehearsals were held in the living room of the Bernsteins' cottage. Thirty young people sprawled across the furniture and spread out on the floor, recalled Shirley, "singing away at the top of their voices to Lenny's direction from the piano."

All for one, and one for all,

Sharing Each success or fall;

All too soon has come the parting

To worldly realms without our wall!

Though we tread lonely byways,

Or embark on princely highways,

We will hear our brother's call,

We will heed our brother's call!

All for one, and one for all;

Sharing Each success or fall;

All too soon has come the parting

To worldly realms without our wall!

School anthem; tercentenary year.

Leonard Bernstein '35.

1935 Class Song, Boston Latin School. Music by Leonard Bernstein, words by Lawrence F. Ebb and Leonard Bernstein.

Lenny the Showman

41

Jennie enjoyed it, even though the kids raided her icebox and left the house in a mess. (Maybe it was better than hearing *Bolero* day after day.) "They all laughed and had fun," she remembered. "When Lenny was around they all followed him." However, when the Sharon Players left ice-cream cups and Fudgsicle sticks all over the furniture and floors, Jennie's "patience was in danger of running out," wrote Burton. "But she was secretly proud."

Sam, however, disapproved. "It was in his way," said Jennie. "He couldn't read the Talmud [a massive compendium of Jewish law and commentaries on the Torah, the first five books in the Bible]. There was too much noise and excitement. The doors were slamming, in and out, in and out. Sam liked quiet, relaxing." On the weekend he shouted at Lenny, "It's *Shabbas* [the Sabbath]! Stop playing the piano and go to *shul* [synagogue]!"

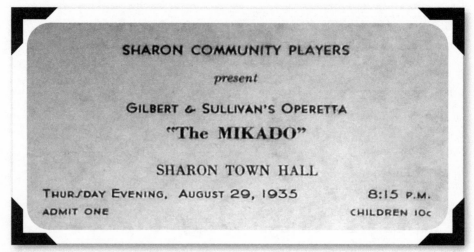

Original ticket for The Mikado, *1935.*

Lenny's little brother, Burtie, who was three years old, loved listening to the rehearsals. He learned the whole score of *The Mikado* while he was supposed to be taking his nap.

The performance took place in the Town Hall auditorium and was a huge success. Admission cost twenty-five cents for adults and ten cents for children. After the players paid for the rental hall, the rest of the profits went to charity. Shirley remembered that each of the players received an honorarium of seventy-five cents. She spent hers on a hot dog, ice cream, and popcorn.

The next summer Lenny and the Sharon Players put on another Gilbert and Sullivan operetta, *H.M.S. Pinafore*. This time they rehearsed at the Town Hall, much to Jennie's relief. But she was not pleased when Lenny discovered the talent of their maid, Lelia Jiampietro. "Lenny had immediately noticed that the new maid sang to herself in a sweet, pure voice while she washed the dishes and swept the floors," recalled Burtie. Lenny "insisted to Jennie that Lelia was born to play Josephine," the leading role of the captain's daughter, who falls in love with a common sailor. He not only convinced Jennie to give the maid time off to go to rehearsals, but he also talked her into allowing them to use Jennie's car as transportation. "So Jennie would stand each morning by the kitchen door, mop in hand, not quite believing the sight that greeted her eyes," remembered Burtie: "at least ten kids in *her* car driving off with *her* maid for the day."

Lenny played the part of Captain Corcoran, Josephine's father. Mildred Spiegel came to Sharon to play Mrs. Cripps (Little Buttercup).

Sharon Players partial cast of "Pinafore," including Shirley Bernstein (middle row, left), Lelia Giampetro (back row, second from left), and Bob Potash (front row, left). Bob's sister Ruth took the photo.

A girl named Ruth Potash accompanied them on the piano. Lenny created a special part for his sister, Shirley, by choreographing "Egyptian Dances," which she performed with her girlfriends, listed on the program as "The Twins Kaplan."

Shirley remembered she drifted out, draped in cheesecloth, and danced to ballet music from the opera *Aida*. But their maid was the star of the show.

The summer ended in a musical triumph for Lenny. His brother, Burton, later wrote, "During Lenny's difficult teens, his most carefree times were the summers spent in Sharon."

5

Lenny at Harvard

Lenny dreamed of music as his life's work. Sam dreamed of turning the Samuel Bernstein Hair Company over to Lenny. But they both agreed on a college education first. Lenny applied to Harvard, because they had a "superb musical department there." Although his grades at Boston Latin had been high and he had graduated *cum laude* [with honors], his chances of being accepted were slim.

In the 1930s there was a quota system at Harvard and other American colleges and universities, which limited the number of Jewish students who could be admitted. At Harvard only a small percentage of the students were Jewish, and anti-Semitism pervaded the school. Nonetheless, Lenny was accepted, partly because of his excellent education at Boston Latin and his good grades, and also because of his many extracurricular musical activities. Despite the high cost of tuition, Sam approved, and Lenny helped pay expenses by winning scholarships and grants.

His friend Sid Ramin was with him when he opened his acceptance letter. "I remember standing on a street corner with him," recalled Sid, "and I said, 'Gee Lenny, you're going to Harvard.' And he said, 'Yes, and I'm going to develop a Harvard accent.' And he did."

In the fall of 1935, when Lenny was seventeen, he entered Harvard as a music major, although Sam hoped that Lenny would "concentrate on something practical like economics." Lenny lived on campus in Wigglesworth dormitory (called Wigg by the students), a residence for freshmen. He had one of three bedrooms adjoining a common living room. Another freshman, Edwin Geller, moved into Wigglesworth and was shocked to see workmen struggling up the stairs with an upright piano. Edwin recalled hoping for quiet roommates, and he prayed that the piano wasn't going to be near his room. But the piano was for Lenny, who had the bedroom right next door.

As always, Lenny liked to play late at night. "We knew it would do no good to complain," said Edwin. Besides, "everyone thought he was a genius and recognized it. Often in the evenings or after dinner he would go into the Freshman Union and perform for hours. There was nothing he couldn't play. You could test him: popular, Gilbert and Sullivan, jazz, the classics—he could do it all, and sing it, too."

In those days popular songs were published as sheet music in offices along so-called Tin Pan Alley, a place in New York City on 28th

Lenny, age eighteen, playing piano in 1936.

Street between Fifth Avenue and Broadway. The demand for sheet music had grown at the beginning of the twentieth century as more and more Americans bought pianos for their homes. Performers were hired to play new songs in music shops along 28th Street. With so many pianos being played at once, the noise sounded as though "hundreds of people were pounding on tin pans," wrote a journalist, and the nickname caught on. Some of Lenny's old favorites, such as "Oh by Jingo," came from Tin Pan Alley, as well as newer hits like "Sweet Georgia Brown" and "Yes, We Have No Bananas."

Harvard Hall in the late 1930s.

Another Harvard freshman, Hal Stubbs, recalled going into the lounge outside the freshman dining hall, hoping to play the piano. "But when I tried a few times after dinner in the evening," he said, "there was always this kid Lenny there ahead of me, and he usually had two or three other guys hanging around listening to him. So I finally settled for joining the audience. He would play all kinds of music—classical, Gilbert & Sullivan, show tunes."

Many popular songs in the 1930s also came from Broadway musicals. When Lenny's friend Sid Ramin visited Harvard each week for a piano lesson with Lenny in his room at Wigglesworth, they played tunes such as "Smoke Gets in Your Eyes" from Jerome Kern's show *Roberta.* "We played a medley of songs from the show," remembered Sid. "Kern was a favorite of ours." Lenny also loved George Gershwin and Cole Porter.

They worked on music theory, too. "Lenny had his own ideas" and carefully wrote down notes. "The problem," said Sid, "was that Lenny was such a fantastic sight reader. I played it by rote. He thought I was reading it. I always used my memory as a crutch." Sid paid a dollar for each lesson and also brought Lenny his favorite candy bar, a Milky Way.

Lenny would have liked to participate in shows at Harvard. But because he was Jewish, he was not invited to join the Hasty Pudding Theatricals, a Harvard revue that put on musicals, and he was not elected to the Signet Society, a student and faculty group interested in the arts. (Years later, in 1957, Lenny was elected an honorary member

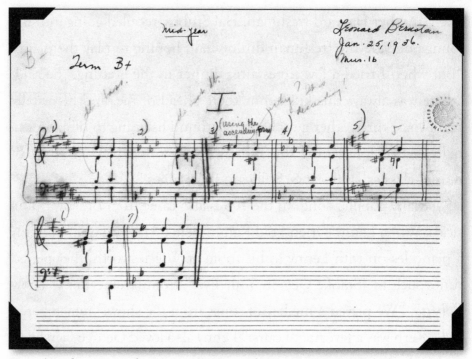

Lenny's midyear exam for Music 1B, Harvard, January 25, 1936.

of the Signet Society as rules changed.) Lenny found other artistic outlets. For a while he accompanied the Glee Club, but they dropped him because he kept arriving late for rehearsals.

At Harvard Lenny took general music courses. The emphasis there was on preparing students to become teachers or musicologists (scholars who research the history and theory of music). "You could not study applied music of any sort," remembered Lenny. He found it strange to "walk through the Music Building for two hours and never hear a note, because it was all on a blackboard or being discussed in hushed whispers."

Lenny's final exam for Music 1B, Harvard, June 5, 1936.

Lenny wanted to perform, so he studied piano outside of school. By now Heinrich Gebhard had accepted him as a student. Sam still refused to pay for the expensive lessons. Lenny earned the money himself by playing at Boston dance parties and teaching students like Sid and children in his old neighborhood when he went back to visit. Often he went to Newton, where the family now lived, to see his mother, sister, and brother. In the new house, he and four-year-old Burtie shared "a big cavernous upstairs bedroom with two huge iron beds." When Lenny came home on weekends, he would enthusiastically tell his little brother about everything he was studying. And he did his laundry and practiced on his piano.

"I could hear him playing the old Chickering downstairs," said Burtie, "the Ravel piano concerto and things. All this became second nature to me."

With Gebhard, Lenny's repertoire grew. That year he worked on Ravel's Concerto in G Major and Gershwin's *Rhapsody in Blue*, as well as compositions by Bach, Beethoven, Brahms, and Debussy. Lenny loved studying with Gebhard. Later he said that his "great piano teacher . . . made every lesson a ride on a magic carpet." They would sit side by side at two pianos. "I would play," said Lenny, "he would play; he would leap up, with that light, deer-like energy, and over my shoulder coax my piano to sing like his. . . . I never once left that studio on my own two feet: I floated out."

6

Genius Boy

Up till now Lenny had thought he would be a concert pianist. He continued classes with Gebhard, and so did his old friend Mildred. When she visited Lenny at Harvard, they played duets of Mendelssohn's *Fingal's Cave* and a Schubert symphony.

A turning point in Lenny's musical life came in January 1937, when he went to a concert with Mildred. That evening Dimitri Mitropoulos, a Greek-born musician who had studied in Berlin, Germany, conducted the Boston Symphony Orchestra. One of the pieces on the program was Respighi's *Toccata for Piano and Orchestra*, which Mitropoulos, an excellent pianist, conducted from the piano. Lenny was "overwhelmed" and went "bananas." Mitropoulos conducted without a baton and used expressive body language to lead the orchestra. He didn't even need a score and knew every piece by heart. Years later Lenny was to imitate his style.

A day or so after the concert, Lenny heard that Mitropoulos would be the guest of honor at a tea given by the Greek Society at Harvard. One version of the story goes that Lenny didn't plan on attending but wound up at the tea accidentally. He had been visiting his parents at home in Newton, and his mother offered to drive him back to Cambridge. While she drove she listened to the radio and tapped in time to the music, as she always did. Distracted, she missed a turn and took Lenny right to the place where the tea was being held. Just then he remembered his invitation and persuaded Jennie to come in with him.

Later, Jennie told it this way: "Mitropoulos was visiting on a Friday night. You know how Jewish mothers cook and bake on Fridays. But Lenny said, 'You must come back to school with me to meet Mitropoulos. He wants to meet me and it has been arranged.' Well. One, two, three, in my housedress we went."

According to all versions Lenny stood in line at the tea to greet Mitropoulos. When it was his turn, Lenny was struck by the conductor's intensity. After formal introductions, Mitropoulos asked Lenny to play the piano for him. First Lenny performed a Chopin nocturne, then one of his own pieces. Mitropoulos must have been impressed, because he invited Lenny to attend rehearsals that week at Symphony Hall.

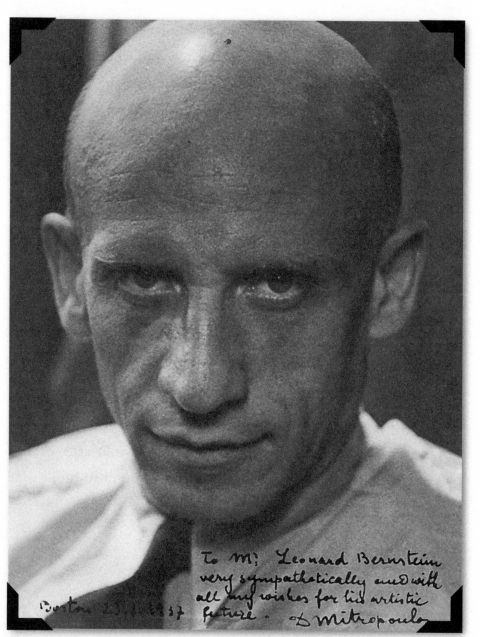

Dimitri Mitropoulos, 1937. The inscription reads, "To Mr. Leonard Bernstein very sympathetically and with all my wishes for his artistic future."

Although it was the week before midterm exams, Lenny went to the rehearsals anyway. He sat in the back row, but when Mitropoulos spotted him, he beckoned Lenny to move up to the front. Then he gave Lenny his own score to follow. "I learned for the first time what a conductor does and how he has to study," said Lenny. "His [Mitropoulos's] memory was incredible; he even rehearsed without a score. . . . He had a passion that at times in rehearsal made him rush into the viola section and grab them by the shoulders and shake them to make them play the way he wanted." Mildred went to one of the rehearsals with Lenny. Afterward Mitropoulos treated them both to lunch and called Lenny a "genius boy." Lenny nearly fainted.

He attended the symphony's concert and following the performance went backstage to the conductor's dressing room. Mitropoulos took him aside and told him he had the talent and ability to be a successful composer. Probably he was responding to Lenny's personality. "You are sensitive in an ideal way," he said. "You must work, work very hard. You must devote all your time to your art. . . . You have everything to make you great; it is up to you only to fulfill your mission."

7

Crazy Artist Nuts

During the summer Lenny usually went to Sharon with his family. But in 1937, he took a summer job for the first time and was the music counselor at Camp Onota in western Massachusetts. There he was known as Uncle Lenny. His job included teaching the boys campfire songs, putting on entertainments for the camp every week, and rehearsing a swing band. Like a Tin Pan Alley musician, Lenny thought of using washtub lids for percussion, since the camp had no drums or cymbals. He created a special arrangement of Gershwin's *Rhapsody in Blue* for the boys that called for a "rhythm band." A photo shows Lenny directing the campers, who sit and stand on the gazebo, his favorite place for staging productions.

Lenny conducting the Camp Onota Rhythm Band, 1937.

On July 11 that summer, the Sunday of Parents' Day weekend, the camp director asked Lenny to play the piano during lunch. At first Lenny refused, because he thought he wouldn't be heard in the noisy mess hall. Then an announcement came over the radio of the sudden death in Los Angeles of George Gershwin. Lenny was shocked and devastated. Gershwin, one of his idols, was only thirty-eight and at the height of his brilliant career as a composer of classical music, the opera *Porgy and Bess*, and many hit Broadway shows. In the middle of lunch, Lenny strode to the piano, sat down, and struck a loud chord. The campers and their parents stopped talking and clinking silverware. When the room was quiet, Lenny announced, "America's greatest

Jewish composer has passed away." Before starting to play Gershwin's Prelude no. 2, he asked that there be no applause. Then Lenny played the soulful piece. When it was over, there was total silence. "As I walked off," said Lenny, "I felt I *was* Gershwin."

George Gershwin.

The highlight that summer was to be a performance of Gilbert and Sullivan's operetta *The Pirates of Penzance*, directed by Lenny. The camp director had hired a talented, unemployed young man from the Bronx to come up and play the part of the Pirate King. His name was Adolph Green.

Adolph was four years older than Lenny and trying to break into show business—without success. He had dropped out of City College of New York and had not had any formal musical training. Yet he was "clever with words and had a phenomenal musical memory." At first Adolph and Lenny were suspicious of each other and gave each other a musical quiz. Lenny sat down at the piano, played a few bars of a piece he said was by Dmitry Shostakovich, and asked Adolph to name it. Adolph said he had never heard of it. Lenny was thrilled, because what he had played was his own composition, *Music for the Dance*, which he had composed for Mildred the previous spring in honor of her twenty-first birthday. Then Adolph asked Lenny to play a piece by Debussy called *Puck*. When Lenny, who claimed he could play anything, admitted he didn't know it, Adolph was equally delighted, because there was no such piece. The two became best friends. They hiked through the hills late at night, singing everything from symphonies (Adolph could imitate every instrument) to funny songs from the 1920s like "I Wish That I'd Been Born in Borneo."

Adolph later recalled, "I knew as we walked and sang and talked, that you, the boy LB, were nothing less than a genius."

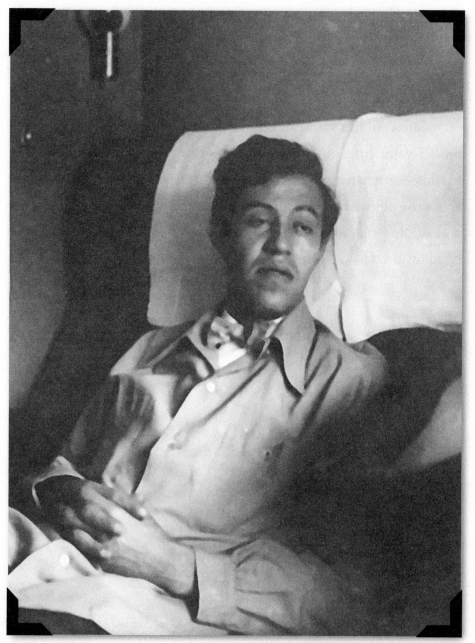

Adolph Green.

Lenny brought Adolph home to the vacation cottage in Sharon to meet his family. The two young men would sit around for hours, quizzing each other on musical subjects and inventing wacky versions of well-known works.

Sam couldn't stand Adolph. "Who is that nut?" he'd say to Jennie. "I want him out of my house." Sam regarded all of Lenny's friends—musicians, poets, writers—as "crazy artist nuts." "He sulked about the house until they departed," remembered Burtie. But Lenny and Adolph remained lifelong friends, and years later they collaborated on Broadway shows.

8

November 14th

When Lenny began his junior year at Harvard in the fall of 1937, he was unsure about his future as a musician. Could he compete as a concert pianist? Was he good enough? He had not been a child prodigy like many superstar pianists, and he was still below the level of successful performers his age.

While in college, Lenny kept studying piano with Gebhard, and Sam kept refusing to pay for the lessons. Sam still "resented Lenny's being serious about a musical career," remembered Lenny's friend Mildred, who also studied with Gebhard. At class they met another of Gebhard's students, Mrs. Robinson, who conducted a State Extension Music Appreciation Course in Haverhill, Massachusetts. "She asked Lenny and me to play the works of the composers she was speaking about," recalled Mildred. "Each Monday night we would board a train and go to a large high school auditorium where the lectures were held." When the course was over, Mrs. Robinson invited them to her country house in New Hampshire. That weekend Lenny took Mildred to an amusement park and insisted they go on the roller coaster. "It was raining and there was thunder and lightning," said Mildred, "but Lenny made me go on it against my will. Sometimes he did crazy things."

On October 31, 1937, Lenny performed the Ravel piano concerto with the State Symphony Orchestra at Sanders Theatre in Cambridge. Newspaper critics attended the concert and gave him great reviews. The *Boston Herald* praised his "genuine talent," and the *Christian Science Monitor* wrote that although he was still in his teens, Lenny played "with an authority and ease which betoken an unusual talent."

Lenny felt encouraged. Perhaps he had a future as a concert pianist. From sophomore year on he lived in Harvard's Eliot House, one of the residence halls for upperclassmen, and enjoyed playing piano in the common room. He also played for screenings of silent films put on by the Harvard Film Society. When they showed the Russian film *Battleship Potemkin*, Lenny performed his own arrangement that included excerpts from *Petrouchka* by the Russian composer Igor Stravinsky and Russian-Jewish folk songs he had learned from Sam.

Lenny did well in his college courses and earned high marks, except for a few Cs in those classes for which he didn't do the work. Classes sometimes bored him, and he filled his notebooks with doodles. On one page he drew variations of the letter *B* and geometric designs in the left margin, along with a stick figure sketch at the bottom.

94

Reading Reading Reading Reading Reading Reading
Reading Reading **Reading** Reading Reading Reading Reading
Bernard Bosanquet: 3 lectures on Aesth^{cs}. nos. 1+2.
A short paper on the use of color pattern in one of the pictures in the
germanic Museum. Also a short comment on a critical
review which was somewhat the aesthetic theory. Before end of
term.

Santayana's two terms; denotation + connotation. As in a jewel,
the first is the actual sensory perception, the second associated,
unsensuous "looks", as an "expensive" look: But this
2nd term is not aesthetic; if it does not come out in the
first term it is aesthetically irrelevant. Because all
this associative material is in the "look" — a Stradivarius
looks impractical, or inexpensive; it may be called aesthetic,
since it is all in the look.

The answer is that if a picture is a representation
of something in life, the lines have fulfilled their function;
This is not so). Representation is not the aim of an
artist or art. Bravo, Mr. Prall! If you hear "There
never was a hillside like that" — say so what!". If there
were such a hillside, it were better to go look at it.

Picture of
Schizophrenia
victim on
hillside full of
cansas stuffed
with Busson's
toenails.

Lenny's doodles, Harvard class notes.

Lenny's cartoons and doodles, including "hollow empty stupid dull uninteresting" (at top), Harvard class notes.

On another page he wrote comments about the course: "hollow empty stupid dull uninteresting." Often he skipped class to practice piano instead.

Harold Shapero, who was two years younger, recalled taking a seminar with Lenny. The class in sixteenth-century counterpoint was taught by Arthur Tillman Merritt, a specialist in Renaissance music. "I did my work," said Harold. "Lenny never showed up." One day the students were supposed to come to class with an original composition based on what they were learning. Lenny composed something entirely different. "He played a little dance piece for Anna Sokolow," a modern dancer he had seen perform in Boston and greatly admired. "It [Lenny's piece] was awful," remembered Harold, "some kind of wild chorus." Their professor said, "'You know, Leonard, this is *not* exactly what we're doing in this class,' and Lenny took his fist and smashed it down and said, 'I like it!'

"His confidence was enormous, gigantic," said Harold. "He didn't worry about making mistakes."

Lenny and Harold liked going to Briggs and Briggs, a music store in Cambridge, to buy sheet music and records. Lenny's friend Mildred remembered that he'd call her on the phone and play the whole record for her that he had just bought.

One day he discovered a recording of *El Salon Mexico* by a new young composer, Aaron Copland. "He couldn't play the record often enough," recalled another friend. Copland, a Jew from Brooklyn, New York, was creating a modern kind of classical music, the "American sound." He wove folk songs and jazz themes into his orchestral works. *El Salon Mexico*, for instance, echoed dance-hall tunes Copland had heard played by a mariachi band on a trip to Mexico.

When Lenny heard a recording of Copland playing his *Piano Variations*, a more serious composition, he "went crazy" about the piece. He described it as "extreme . . . fiercely dissonant, intoxicating." Since he couldn't afford to buy the sheet music, he persuaded his philosophy professor, David Prall, a music fan, to buy it for him. Lenny and other students had become friends with the professor. "His rooms were a place for us to go," said Lenny. "And he [Prall] also bought himself a little piano," recalled Lenny, "so that I could play it for him." In exchange for the gift, Lenny wrote an essay about the *Variations* for the professor's course.

Lenny took the music to his piano teacher, Gebhard. Gebhard said if Lenny could teach it to him, he'd "teach it back to Lenny." After that, Lenny played Copland's *Piano Variations* constantly. This loud, startling, unmelodic piece became his "trademark," he recalled. "I could be relied upon to empty any room in Boston within three minutes by sitting down at the piano and starting it."

In November of Lenny's junior year at Harvard, he and a fellow student went to Anna Sokolow's New York debut. With another friend, poet Muriel Rukeyser, they sat in the first row of the balcony. "Already in his seat on my right," remembered Lenny, "was an odd-looking man in his thirties, a pair of glasses resting on his great hooked nose and a mouth filled with teeth flashing a wide grin at Muriel. She leaned

Aaron Copland at the piano.

across to greet him, then introduced us: 'Aaron Copland . . . Leonard Bernstein.'" Lenny was so excited he nearly fell out of the balcony.

That date, November 14, happened to be Aaron's birthday. At the end of the dance recital, he invited Lenny and his friends to come to his loft for a party. Lenny was thrilled. *"Aaron Copland's famous loft! Where he worked!"* At the party Lenny told Copland that he was a great fan and that he knew the *Piano Variations*. Aaron dared him to play it. Lenny said, "It'll ruin your party."

"Not *this* party," said Aaron.

"So I played it," said Lenny, "and they were all—Aaron particularly—drop-jawed. And it did not empty the room." Aaron praised Lenny and said, "I wish I could play it like that." Then, recalled Lenny, "I followed the *Variations* with every piece I could remember. . . . I must have stayed at the piano for hours."

From that night on, the two became good friends. Lenny never forgot the date of Aaron's birthday, because it marked one of the most important events of his life. Whenever Aaron came to Boston, he stayed in the guest quarters of Eliot House, which Lenny arranged for him. And whenever Lenny came down to New York from Harvard, he'd visit Aaron and show him whatever music he had been composing: a two-piano piece, a string quartet, a violin sonata. Aaron critiqued the work. "This is good; these two bars are good," he'd say. "Take these two bars and start from there."

Later Lenny said, "Aaron became the closest thing to a composition teacher I ever had."

Lenny's string trio sketch, written in pencil in the Student's Music Pad notebook,
November 30, 1937.

Aaron believed that Lenny had potential as a composer. Yet Lenny still wondered if he would achieve his dream of a career in music. What exactly would he do? How would he break into a field dominated by Europeans? Perhaps he would wind up working for the Samuel Bernstein Hair Company after all. When he expressed his worries, Aaron giggled, then said, "Stop complaining. You are destined for success."

9

Glimmering Possibility

Despite Aaron's support and confidence in him, Lenny still had doubts about his future. What kind of musical work would he do?

In the fall Dimitri Mitropoulos returned to the United States to become the principal conductor of the Minneapolis Symphony Orchestra. Lenny wrote to him. In the spring of 1938 Mitropoulos responded by paying for a train ticket so that Lenny could join him when he would be conducting an all-Wagner program with soloists from the New York Metropolitan Opera. During that week in Minneapolis, Lenny spent hours in the conductor's greenroom, sight-reading orchestral scores. Mitropoulos recognized Lenny's extraordinary abilities—not only as a creator of music, but also possibly as a conductor. Mitropoulos promised to give Lenny a job with the Minneapolis Symphony as soon as he graduated. When Lenny came back to

Boston, he said to his father, "Papa, I'm going to make music my life." Sam was probably not happy to hear this news.

The thought of becoming a conductor had not entered Lenny's mind before. Now it seemed like a "glimmering possibility."

A year later, in April 1939, he made his conducting debut at Harvard with the Greek Society production of Aristophanes' *The Birds*. Lenny had composed music for the play. One of the movements included the whole cast whistling the song "Me and My Shadow." His piano teachers Heinrich Gebhard and Miss Coates came to the performance, as well as his friend and mentor, Aaron Copland.

In a letter of congratulations, Miss Coates wrote, "I really feel you have a great gift for conducting."

For his senior thesis Lenny wrote a paper titled "The Absorption of Race Elements into American Music." He discussed his two favorite composers, Gershwin and Copland, and how they had used jazz and Latin American influences to create a new, modern kind of American music. "The greatest single racial influence upon American music as a whole has been that of the Negroes [African Americans]," he wrote. "The earliest adaptations of Negro material by American composers made use of the rhythms, above all." Lenny traced the history of music in America from hymns, spirituals, and folk songs to "Negro themes," "swing," and popular songs from Tin Pan Alley. He spent months working on the paper and wrote to Aaron, "What music of other composers in America would support my point, and where can I get hold of it? . . . You see, I know and hear so little American stuff."

Aaron replied, "Composing in this country is still pretty young no matter how you look at it."

Lenny submitted his thirty-thousand-word thesis in April 1939, "in partial fulfillment for the degree with honors of Bachelor of Arts." He graduated from Harvard *cum laude* in June 1939, when he was

Lenny in cap and gown for Harvard graduation, 1939.

almost twenty-one. He didn't know what to do next. Should he concentrate on piano playing? Or was he gifted enough to become a composer? Perhaps a conductor, as Mitropoulos had suggested?

"The idea of conducting seemed very glamorous and remote, and . . . impossible," said Lenny. But there was no word from Mitropoulos, and a potential summer job at Mills College in California had fallen through.

He wrote to a friend who had graduated from Harvard the previous year, "No money, no practicing, no ideas."

10

Me? A Conductor?

In June 1939, when Lenny graduated from Harvard, the world was in chaos. War threatened in Europe as the Nazis rose to power under the leadership of Adolf Hitler. Now Sam felt sure that Lenny would be glad to have a secure position with the Bernstein Hair Company. He offered Lenny a job at a salary of one hundred dollars a week. Lenny turned him down.

Instead he accepted an invitation from Adolph Green to come to New York for the summer and share his sublet apartment. Sam thought that once Lenny had a taste of the risky life of a big-city musician, he'd be only too happy to return to Boston and join the family business. So he gave Lenny "barely enough money" to sustain him over the summer for "one last fling," remembered Burtie.

Adolph lived downtown in Greenwich Village and had a "glorious Steinway grand" that Lenny played at all hours of the night and day. There were "violent complaints by the landlord and some of the neighbors," he wrote to Miss Coates. "Please pray for me so that I can get a good job and find a good penthouse to live in far from the madding crowd, where I can bang away to my heart's content."

The only job Lenny found was occasionally accompanying Adolph's nightclub act. Adolph performed with four other unknowns in a group that called themselves the Revuers. They put on witty satirical sketches with songs and dances at a club in the Village. The first time Lenny saw the show he loved it. After the last performance, "around 3:00 a.m., he got to the piano and started to play," recalled Betty Comden, one of the Revuers. "And we were there till six or seven in the morning, with him playing away, everything, Bach, Beethoven, Brahms, and finally boogie-woogie. That night I was so staggered by this marvelous man, this kid . . . and I knew that just knowing him would affect my life. I went home and I shook my mother—I woke her up—and I said, 'Mom, I've met my first genius,' and she said, 'Oh, that's nice,' and went back to sleep."

Despite Lenny's success with his pals, he had no regular work. By late August, with only four dollars in his pocket—which he spent on a clarinet in a pawnshop—he returned to Sharon. "I went home to Massachusetts with my tail between my legs," he wrote.

While sitting around the house, Lenny heard the news.

On September 1, 1939, the Nazis invaded Poland, and war broke

Lenny talking with Adolph Green (background). Betty Comden is typing while choreographer Jerome Robbins looks over her shoulder.

out in Europe. Sam worried about his elderly parents, Dinah and Yudel, who were still living in Russian Ukraine by choice. They would be "prime victims" of the Nazis, who were known to persecute the Jews. Sam hadn't seen his mother and father for thirty-two years and wanted to bring them to America as soon as possible. He read the news reports from Germany and listened to the radio. "Sometimes

Sam would want to discuss the grim events of the day with his family— or lecture on them at Sunday afternoon dinner," remembered Burtie.

Meanwhile Lenny received an unexpected phone call from Mitropoulos that week, asking him to come to New York right away. Lenny had no money, so that very night he persuaded a friend to drive him down. In the morning, according to Lenny, he met with Mitropoulos, who asked him what he had been doing. "I've finished Harvard," said Lenny. "I've studied the piano all along . . . and I'm playing pretty well. I write music. But I can't find a job. . . . What shall I do?"

And Mitropoulos said to him, "I know what you should do. You must be a conductor."

Although he had never seen Lenny conduct, he knew from their talks and from the week they had spent together in Minneapolis that Lenny had the "gifts"—exceptional musicality—needed for the task. Now Lenny said, "Me? A conductor?" Then he said, "Fine, well, how does one become one?"

And Mitropoulos said, "You study."

Lenny said, "Where do you study conducting?"

"There's the Juilliard School," said Mitropoulos, and he recommended a particular teacher.

Juilliard was in New York. Lenny called to apply but was told that the class was already filled.

Another version of the story goes that Lenny had already been to Juilliard seeking a conducting fellowship but found that he was a month too late to apply. He sent Aaron Copland a letter asking for help. "Can something be done?" he wrote. "Or do I turn in desperation to the possibility of Curtis?"

The conductor in charge of conducting classes at the Curtis Institute of Music in Philadelphia was Fritz Reiner, another friend of Aaron's. Dr. Reiner, much respected and feared, was a Hungarian Jew who had conducted the opera company in Dresden, Germany, before coming to the United States in 1922 to take over the Cincinnati Symphony. "Any day on which he failed to lose his temper," remarked an observer, "was a day in which he was actually too sick to conduct." In 1931 Dr. Reiner had begun teaching at Curtis in addition to conducting the Pittsburgh Symphony. Aaron gave Lenny tips about meeting Reiner after one of his concerts, to get on his good side, and Lenny carefully followed Aaron's advice.

Lenny's version of the story went that it was Mitropoulos who said he had heard that Fritz Reiner had formed a class for conductors at the Curtis Institute. It would start in October. Dr. Reiner agreed to give Lenny a special audition in late September.

Lenny hurriedly began to prepare. With borrowed money he bought two scores, Beethoven's Seventh Symphony and Rimsky-Korsakov's *Scheherazade*, and tried to memorize them for the test. "I had never really studied orchestral scores from the point of view of conducting them," he said. So he asked Aaron to help him. Lenny took a train to Woodstock, New York, where Aaron was renting a house, and over the weekend they worked together. Aaron had a couple of cats.

Lenny was highly allergic to cats, and at that time of year he also suffered from hay fever. By the time he arrived in Philadelphia for his audition, he was wheezing and his eyes were swollen and watering. "I could barely see out of my eyes," he remembered. "I was coughing and sneezing and there was this very gruff, tough man called Fritz Reiner, who sort of grunted and said hmmm. And he took a big score and put it on the piano, opening it to the middle—he wouldn't let me see the title."

Dr. Reiner said to Lenny, "Do you know that piece?"

Lenny stared at the black notes and admitted that he didn't. Then Dr. Reiner said, "Do you think you can play it on the piano?"

Lenny shivered and said he would try. "I was lucky," he recalled. "Some heavenly fire took hold of me, opened my hayfeverish [sic] eyes, and I played it like a maniac. Suddenly I realized I was playing a tune that sounded like a folk song [in this case, a famous student song from the University of Breslau in Germany] that we had sung in grammar school years before.

> "What clatters on the roof
> With quick, impatient hoof?
> I think it must be Santa Claus,
> Dear old Santa Claus."

Something clicked in Lenny's head. He remembered having heard the piece on the radio years before, recognizing the tune, and hearing the announcer say, "That was the *Academic Festival Overture* by Brahms."

Dr. Fritz Reiner. The inscription reads, "For Leonard Bernstein with sincere good wishes."

So now he turned to Dr. Reiner and confidently said, "Of course I know this piece," and named it. And he was accepted into the conducting class.

Lenny rushed home to Boston to announce the good news. Sam was not pleased, Shirley recalled. He thought it was pointless for Lenny to go to Curtis. In those days the symphony orchestras in America were all led by older conductors who had been born and trained in Europe. Fritz Reiner, then fifty-one years old, conducted the Pittsburgh Symphony Orchestra. Russian-born Serge Koussevitzky, sixty-five years old, led the Boston Symphony Orchestra. John Barbirolli, a forty-year-old Englishman, led the New York Philharmonic. And of course, Dimitri Mitropoulos, then forty-three years old, directed the Minneapolis Symphony Orchestra. The doors were closed to a young American, no matter how well trained and qualified.

Sam thought Lenny didn't have a chance of succeeding. "Not one more cent for music," he said at first. But Lenny, at age twenty-one, borrowed money, packed up, kissed the family goodbye, and took off for Philadelphia.

11

Work and Work and Work

Lenny described Philadelphia as a "city of dust and grit and horror." But now he was convinced that conducting was his calling, and Curtis seemed the right school where he could learn. Students received scholarships to cover tuition. However, there were no dorms, and Lenny had to find a place to live—and pay for that as well as food.

Sam thought Curtis was a big mistake. However, Lenny used his "ultimate powers of persuasion" and talked his father into giving him his blessing and "some expense money," recalled Burtie. Lenny said, "My father gave me $40 a month to live on, barely enough to pay my room rent at one of the boardinghouses they had for Curtis students."

Fritz Reiner conducting the Curtis Institute of Music student orchestra at a dress rehearsal.

Dimitri Mitropoulos sent Lenny a check for $225 to help out with expenses. In a postcard he wrote, "I feel happy that everything seems to be welcoming you in this school, in spite of the pessimistic warnings of Mr. Reiner."

Dr. Reiner came to Curtis only one day a week from Pittsburgh to teach. He expected his students to know whole scores by heart and be familiar with the parts of every instrument. In the middle of a rehearsal, he would stop and ask a frightened student what the second clarinet was playing at that exact moment. "It looks like a long up-hill climb," Lenny wrote in his first letter to his piano teacher in Boston, Miss Coates. "But I proceed nothing daunted, despite all the venomous attacks I hear on all sides against Mr. Reiner, with whom I am studying."

Once Lenny made the mistake of calling his teacher "Fritz." In a frosty tone Dr. Reiner responded, "Yes, Mr. Bernstein." Dr. Reiner's students were allowed to conduct only once or twice a term, since the faculty believed that the student orchestra would get better training by playing under the direction of a professional conductor.

The Curtis Institute was a center for talented young kids—child prodigies. Lenny later described his fellow pupils as "still in short pants." When he auditioned for Rudolf Serkin, the head of the piano department, he passed. But Lenny couldn't study with him. "I seem to be over age (!)" he wrote to Miss Coates. "They've tentatively allotted him a chap of 16 and a girl of 13, so that he can *mould* them," he joked. So Lenny was assigned to Madame Isabelle Vengerova, whom he described as "the greatest piano teacher in America, better than Serkin." The Russian-born teacher was demanding. "She is a veritable slave driver, with a passion for *detailed* perfection," he wrote. "Nothing less will please her." At Lenny's first lesson with Madame Vengerova, he played the Bach fugue he had performed for his audition. She stopped him after a few bars and said, "Why are you banging that way? Why are you kicking the pedal? Why is the pedal down at all? You're playing Bach."

"She scared the living daylight out of me," wrote Lenny, "so I left the lesson absolutely trembling!"

In more letters to Miss Coates, he described his new teacher's methods. "It seems she is trying to make me relax for one thing, to end my 'percussive' touch. . . . And she actually drives me during lessons so that I'm exhausted after them. Well, that's what I've been told I needed—a teacher of iron—with no sense of humor, who will make a controlled pianist of me."

A fellow student, seventeen-year-old Lukas Foss, said that Vengerova insisted on practice. "She would have a heart attack if we came to her class unprepared," he recalled.

Curtis provided Lenny with a Steinway grand so that he could practice in his room. "It's a dream of a piano," he wrote to Miss Coates in a note thanking her for brownies she had sent. "I work and work and work (practice about 3 to 5 hrs. a day), and do nothing else, except sleep plenty." Like other students, he lived in a boardinghouse near the school. Lenny's ugly room without a bath was above a delicatessen.

Madame Isabelle Vengerova.

At first Lenny had no friends at Curtis. The other students disliked him because he was the only one who had gone to college. "They regarded me as a Harvard smart aleck, an intellectual big shot, a snob, a show-off," he recalled. "I know this to be true because they later told me so." Lenny even had "official enemies. There was actually a secret anti-Bernstein club," he said. They thought he was a "fake" because he could sight-read complicated orchestral scores so readily. "They were convinced that I had secretly prepared them and then passed them off as sight-reading."

One of his few friends was the director of the Curtis Institute, composer Randall Thompson. He too was a Harvard graduate and had lectured there. At Curtis, Lenny studied orchestration with him. They discovered that they both enjoyed doing crossword puzzles, and Thompson introduced Lenny to the more difficult British crossword puzzles. "I just adore doing them," said Lenny, "because they check out *right*. . . . It's the only thing in the world that is. Except music!"

Lenny also became friends with another piano student, Phyllis Moss. She thought he was lonely during his early days at Curtis. "I remember taking walks around Philadelphia with him and he poured his heart out," she recalled. Yet Lukas Foss remembered, "he never struck me as miserable. I remember saying to him that he had such an expansive, luxurious way of being miserable that it didn't seem miserable to me."

During Lenny's first winter at Curtis, he met a girl named Shirley Gabis in the delicatessen downstairs from his room, and they became

Dr. Randall Thompson and a class in orchestration. Lenny is third from left.

Shirley Gabis.

friends. "Lenny was at the counter, wearing a coat that looked ten sizes too big for him, as if he had inherited it," she remembered.

Soon Shirley and Lenny began meeting at Delancey Pharmacy, a local hangout for Curtis students where they could buy a tuna fish sandwich and a cup of coffee for fifteen cents. Shirley was only a junior in high school, but she loved music. She took Lenny home to meet her mother, and her mother enjoyed his company, too. Shirley's grandfather had been a dealer in phonograph records, and at her home they still had shelves of pop music from the 1920s. "Lenny would tear through the songs at the piano singing at the top of his lungs," she remembered. Once he came over to her apartment with a photocopied, accordion-pleated score of Aaron Copland's *Billy the Kid*. "After we played it four-hands," she recalled, "he unfolded the score all the way down the three flights of stairs. That was the same day he stamped his foot so hard on the floor while he was playing the Copland *Variations* that the chandelier fell in the apartment below. My mother got a letter from the landlord saying that this was the last straw and that we would have to move. We did."

Lenny in Rittenhouse Square, Philadelphia.

When Lenny's father came to Philadelphia for a visit, he met Shirley's mother. She owned a beauty parlor, so they had much in common. Sam told her that he didn't understand why Lenny wanted to be a musician when he could "make a hundred dollars a week with free room and board by working for him in the beauty supply business."

But Lenny continued his studies. In the spring of 1940, he read that Serge Koussevitzky, conductor of the Boston Symphony Orchestra, was starting a new school for young musicians at Tanglewood, a summer performance center in Lenox, Massachusetts, that the orchestra had opened three years earlier. The school, called the Berkshire Music Center, would offer a variety of courses, including conducting classes taught by Koussevitzky himself.

Koussevitzky, born in Russia, had come to the United States in 1924 to conduct the Boston Symphony Orchestra. He had a passion for new music and championed American composers such as Aaron Copland. Koussevitzky dreamed of establishing a school for talented music students in the United States where they could begin their professional lives. America had only five or six good orchestras in those days, recalled Shirley Bernstein. The few opportunities in those orchestras usually went to Europeans who, like Koussevitsky, had come to America. He wanted to give American musicians a chance to train as apprentices.

Teenagers and young adults from all over the country applied. So did Lenny. Armed with letters of recommendation from Aaron

Serge Koussevitzky, September 25, 1943. The inscription reads, "To my very dear Lenushka, with all my faith, hope, and love."

Copland, who was going to be on the faculty, and Fritz Reiner, plus a telegram from Mitropoulos, Lenny met Koussevitzky at Symphony Hall in Boston. "There I was sitting in the presence of the great Koussevitzky, trembling and white," remembered Lenny. "And suddenly Koussevitzky said, 'But of course I vill take you in my class.' It was just like that. A great shock. A wonderful shock."

In July Lenny went to Tanglewood and loved it. "Such an explosion in my life," he recalled. The school gave him a scholarship of fifty dollars and paid half of his room fee. Lenny earned the rest. He lived in Room 57 of a prep school run by Jesuits and used by the Tanglewood students during the summer. His four roommates included Harold Shapero, the young composer he had known at Harvard, and a violinist, a cellist, and a clarinetist. Harold wrote a work for clarinet, cello, and violin that he called *Room 57*. He remembered Lenny sitting at his desk in the corner, shouting and yelling as he prepared to rehearse Rimsky-Korsakov's *Scheherazade*. "Their room was by far the noisiest at Tanglewood," recalled a dormmate.

Lenny, Lukas Foss (his fellow conducting and piano student from Curtis), and three others worked with Koussevitzky in a special class. Each day began with movement lessons. Koussevitzky hired a leading ballet dancer to help the student conductors learn how to walk, bow, and be graceful on the podium. They practiced in a room lined with mirrors so they could see themselves. "I did this just one day by myself," recalled Lenny, "and fell about in such laughter that I couldn't repeat it." He didn't worry about how he looked while conducting.

Koussevitsky's birthday tea, Berkshire Music Center, 1940. From left to right: Lenny, Lukas Foss, and Serge Koussevitsky.

Lenny conducting Stravinsky's L'Historie de Soldat *at an informal tea party, Tanglewood, August 1940. Koussevitsky and his wife, Natalie, look down from the balcony. The inscription is to Helen Coates.*

Koussevitzky agreed and, after the first week's lessons, canceled the dance class for all the student conductors.

Lenny formed a particularly close friendship with Koussevitzky. "He became like a surrogate father to me," said Lenny. "He had no children of his own and I had a father whom I loved very much but who was not for this musical thing at all. . . . And there was something about his being Russian that was terribly moving and close to me. I didn't know Russian and I had not met many Russians but my parents had been born in Russia [Ukraine]."

Kouss, as Lenny privately referred to him, conducted with a baton and wanted Lenny to do the same. Lenny preferred using only his hands, like Mitropoulos. Kouss pleaded with Lenny to conduct with the little baguette, as he called it. "Look, it's like a pencil," he said to Lenny. But Lenny refused. Conducting music with his hands related more to playing the piano and felt right.

At Curtis, Lenny rarely had the chance to conduct the student orchestra. At Tanglewood, however, he started conducting right away. His first performance was on July 12, 1940. Excitedly he wrote home to his family.

Dearest Folks—

I've been conducting the orchestra every morning, & I'm playing my first concert tomorrow night. Kouss gave me the hardest & longest number of all . . . as my first performance. And Kouss is so pleased with my work. . . . He told me he is convinced that I have a wonderful gift, & he is already

making me a great conductor. . . . The orchestra likes me
very much, best of all the conductors, & responds so
beautifully in rehearsal. Of course, the concert tomorrow
night (Shabbas, yet!) will tell whether I can keep my head
in performance, . . . I wish you could all be here—it's so
important to me. . . . [I]f it goes well there's no telling what
may happen . . .

Please come up—I think I'll be conducting every Friday
night . . .

All my love—
Lenny

"When Sam finally drove Jennie, Shirley, and me to Tanglewood from Sharon," recalled Burtie, "it was obvious that everything Lenny had said in his letter was true. The place seemed to have been invented for him alone."

Sam felt jealous of Koussevitzky for being a second father to Lenny, Burtie remembered. Sam knew that Koussevitzky had converted from Judaism to Christianity to further his musical career. Would he encourage Lenny to do the same? Koussevitzky had already suggested to Lenny that a better name for a conductor would be Leonard S. (for Samuelovitch, son of Sam) Burns. But Lenny kept his own name.

By the end of the summer, Lenny faced a dilemma. Koussevitzky had invited him to study with him in Boston that winter instead of returning to Curtis. Lenny wrote to Mitropoulos and asked for his

Lenny, at right, and his friends joking around at Tanglewood, 1940.

advice. Mitropoulos wrote back that perhaps Lenny might not need any further training at Curtis.

But when Fritz Reiner heard about it, he was furious and probably exchanged sharp words with Koussevitzky. The school didn't want to lose its most brilliant conducting pupil. On October 1 Lenny received a telegram from Kouss: "Learn [sic] from Dr. Randall Thompson that your scholarship at Curtis Institute extends another year. Honestly believe you must complete your obligation."

To lure him back, Curtis even offered Lenny free lunches. So at age twenty-two, he returned to Philadelphia.

12

What to Do Next?

As soon as Lenny arrived in Philadelphia in October 1940, he registered for the draft. It seemed likely that the United States would enter the war, and young men were obligated to sign up for the armed services. Lenny was turned down and marked 4-F, physically unfit, because of his chronic asthma. In a way he felt grateful, because he could continue his studies. "On the other hand," he wrote, "it was a bit depressing not to be able to take part in this war; but I felt: I don't like wars at all."

Sam was overjoyed that Lenny was rejected by the draft board. In Yiddish he cried out, "Thanks be to God my son won't have to go to war."

Sam's parents, Dinah and Yudel, and his sister Sura-Rivka and her family were still in Russian Ukraine, and he was trying desperately to make arrangements to get them to America. Sam exchanged letters with his brother, Shlomo, who lived in Moscow and didn't want to leave. Neither did Sura-Rivka. But Sam's parents were in danger. His younger sister, Clara, who had given Lenny his first piano, offered to take care of Dinah and Yudel in her Orthodox community in Brooklyn. So in the winter of 1940, while Lenny was at Curtis, his paternal grandparents sailed from Leningrad to New York on a ship "under neutral colors."

Meanwhile Lenny struggled to earn enough money for living expenses. This year he had a larger, better room. He even had his own bathroom with a tub. Occasionally he got jobs playing piano through a booking agency at Curtis. The booking agent, Thomas ("Tod") Perry, not only arranged performances for Lenny but also lent him his white tie and tails when formal clothing was required. Tod was four inches taller, but Lenny appreciated the loan. They had become friends the previous summer at Tanglewood. Lenny also gave piano lessons to kids he called "rich brats" for five dollars an hour, and he coached a boys' chorus at a private school.

That fall Lenny transcribed Aaron Copland's *El Salon Mexico* for piano for a fee of twenty-five dollars. He sent Aaron a "clean copy," but it was not in good enough shape. "Your idea of a manuscript 'ready for the printer' is to weep," Aaron wrote to Lenny. "I'm preparing one of my best lectures for you on said subject. We need a couple of hours to talk over several points." The piece was eventually published in 1941, and it was the first time Lenny's name appeared on a music publication.

Lenny and Aaron Copland at the piano, around 1940.

Lenny's own studies went well. Although he nicknamed his piano teacher "La Tirana" ("the tyrant"), he later said that she "was a very great teacher." In his conducting classes he still found Reiner difficult. "He demanded total knowledge," said Lenny. "You had no right to step up on that podium unless you knew everything about what every member of the orchestra had to do." Lenny agreed with him, and adopted Reiner's high standards as his own.

Eventually Lenny and Reiner became friends. "It was hard going," said Lenny, "because he was not basically a friendly man, being so demanding and severe." Kouss, on the other hand, was warm and taught in a way that Lenny described as "inspirational."

Lenny finished his second year at Curtis with many triumphs. On April 26, 1941, he made his first radio broadcast as a conductor, leading the Institute Orchestra in Brahms's A Major Serenade. His former piano teacher, Miss Coates, heard the broadcast in Boston and sent him a postcard with the message, *"Bravo!—a thousand times!"* The program was repeated at Curtis, with Reiner conducting and Lenny playing the piano. On April 30 Lenny performed in a program given by Madame Vengerova's graduating pupils. In May he received his diploma from Curtis and graduated with outstanding grades—A+ for piano and A in conducting, supposedly the only A Reiner ever gave to a student.

That summer Lenny hurried back to Tanglewood for another glorious season. He was one of six conducting pupils who studied with Kouss. Tuesday through Friday they rehearsed for three hours in the

Curtis Institute Class of 1941. Lenny is in the middle row, fourth from left.

morning, and they gave a concert every Friday night. Lenny recalled that members of the conducting class would play piano for one another for a particular piece. "Lukas Foss would play the piano while I conducted," he said, "and I would play while he conducted. It was quite an interesting class . . . with authentic geniuses like Lukas Foss." In addition to the student orchestra, the Boston Symphony Orchestra performed during the last three weeks, drawing audiences of thousands.

Lenny described his first concert in a letter to his friend Mildred, who was studying piano in New York. He had conducted *American Festival Overture* by his friend William Schuman, a contemporary composer he had met through Aaron Copland. The overture was a modern piece with unusual harmonies, challenging to listeners.

"It [the overture] brought down the house," he wrote. "Screaming, cheering, ovation. Kouss kissed me in public. Bill Schuman was there himself and said he never heard such a performance of anything before. Aaron was hopping around like a duck, and I got two more bows than Kouss had gotten."

At the end of his letter, Lenny added, "God, I sound conceited, but it was really marvelous that you can play a piece of modern American music full of bitonality and whatnot, and people at the end scream 'Bravo.'"

The Tanglewood season closed with a gala benefit to raise money for the United Service Organizations (USO) and British Relief. By this time it seemed inevitable that the United States would soon enter the war.

In August Lenny went home to Sharon. His father kept a map of Europe on the wall with different colored pins marking the advances and retreats of various armies. "The black pins, representing the Nazis, were well into the Ukraine [Russia]," remembered Burtie. "The red pins, the Russians, were retreating east toward Moscow." One day they heard a report on the radio about a fierce battle fought in Shepetovka, a town near the *shtetl* where Jennie had been born. Although Sam and Jennie had no close relatives in the town, they had many family members in the area and worried about them. "If the stories of summary executions of Polish and Russian Jews were true," said Burtie, "they didn't stand a chance. As despised as Hitler was in 1941, nobody could bring himself to believe the stories were absolutely true. Such total evil was impossible."

Lenny with Koussevitzky at Tanglewood, 1941.

Lenny at Tanglewood, around 1941.

In August, Sam's mother, Dinah, came to Sharon to stay with them. It was a nightmare. Her husband, Sam's father, had died the winter before, and she blamed it on America. Since Dinah was extremely Orthodox, they had to make their house perfect for her needs. For instance, Lenny was not allowed to play piano on the Sabbath. "My family—indeed, the whole Lake Avenue community—was scrubbed, sanctified, and purified when Sam drove up in his Oldsmobile, his mother next to him on the front seat," recalled Burtie.

Lenny and Shirley had trouble communicating with their grandmother. "They tried, in desperation, sign language, Latin, French—anything," said Burtie. Only their mother, Jennie, seemed able to connect with her. But Dinah complained about everything and drove everyone crazy, even her son Sam. Later in life Lenny wrote a duet for Sam and Dinah that began, "Try, Dinah, try to be kind. . . ." Finally they arranged to have her stay with cousins in Roxbury, a suburb of Boston where they had once lived.

Sam had sold the big house in Newton because business was not as good as it had been. A new cold-wave permanent had come on the market, making his permanent-wave machine obsolete. So he converted the house in Sharon to make it comfortable year-round.

Lenny sat around, wondering what to do next. He had received a questionnaire from the Army. Although he still suffered from asthma and hay fever, he thought he might be called up and examined again, and he planned to say that his asthma attacks only rarely occurred. When Koussevitzky asked him to stay in Boston to work part-time as his assistant, Lenny wrote, "I cannot be given a responsible position while there is the probability of my being suddenly taken away from it to join the Army." In closing he wrote, "I wonder if I might be of service in the USO where I could simultaneously serve national defense and remain in my field of endeavor [music]."

When Lenny went for his medical interview, however, he was once again classified as 4-F because of his asthma.

Kouss tried without success to arrange for Lenny to do music work with the armed services. So Lenny remained in Boston to play scores for Kouss and give him advice on new pieces that were submitted to him for performances. "Modern music is becoming so crazy," said Kouss to Lenny, "and you young people understand it but I don't." He presented Lenny with a new piano concerto by Carlos Chávez, the Mexican composer, and said, "How would you like to play the piano part with the Boston Symphony?"

Lenny was thrilled and practiced for three months. But when he was ready to perform, he was told he couldn't because he belonged to the union, the Boston branch of the American Federation of Musicians. At that time the Boston Symphony Orchestra was still a non-union orchestra, but Lenny had a union card. "I had to have one in order to do other little gigs and jobs around Boston, and that disentitled me to work with the Boston Symphony," he recalled.

Once again Sam offered him a job in the Samuel Bernstein Hair Company at a starting salary of $100 a week and with free room and board. It would give Sam *nachas*, the Jewish principle of pleasure from the achievement of a child, to have "a well-tutored son take over the family business.

"But he wanted music," said Sam. "So I got him a studio . . . and had a piano put in it for him."

According to Burtie, Lenny "wangled enough money out of Sam to rent a drafty studio on Huntington Avenue."

Lenny sent out announcements offering his services as a piano teacher. "I thought that would help me support myself," he said. Only one pupil showed up, a man named Bernie who drove in once a week

December 5, 1941

• **LEONARD BERNSTEIN**

Announces the opening of his studio
for the teaching of   .   .   .   .
PIANO and MUSICAL ANALYSIS

295 HUNTINGTON AVE., BOSTON
Room 403   **Gainsboro Building**

KENmore 4364

Announcement of the opening of Lenny's studio.

from Worcester. Sam felt sure that Lenny's venture would fail—"making Lenny a candidate once again for his business just a couple of miles away—and Sam was right," recalled Burtie. Lenny opened his studio on December 5, 1941. Two days later the Japanese fleet attacked Pearl Harbor, and the United States entered the war.

"Nobody was interested in arts or anything of the sort at that point," said Lenny.

"He was a twenty-three-year-old trained and promising musician with no place to go," wrote Burtie.

13

On the Town

In the summer of 1942, Lenny returned to Tanglewood as Kouss's assistant in his conducting class. Because of the war, the Boston Symphony Orchestra didn't perform that summer, but Kouss decided to hold a festival using the student orchestra. "It was magnificent," remembered Lenny. They played works such as Dmitry Shostakovich's Fifth Symphony. Despite gas rationing, people in Lenox and the Berkshires "turned out in thousands." They shared cars, hitched lifts, and even hired hay wagons to bring them to the concerts.

"At the end of that summer," said Lenny, "I decided I would not go back to Boston and try and give piano lessons or anything but I would—yet once again—seek my fortune in New York."

Lenny moved back to "the Big City" in September and "looked everywhere for a job." Any job. He played piano for dance classes in studios at the top of Carnegie Hall, he gave lessons for a dollar an hour, he coached vocalists, and he performed for the soldiers at Fort Dix, New Jersey. But that didn't bring in enough money. In desperation he wrote to Aaron Copland, who was in Hollywood, California, scoring music for movies, and asked for advice. Aaron suggested that he try getting nightclub work. Lenny got in touch with his old friend Adolph Green and occasionally accompanied his act, the Revuers. Through Adolph, Lenny had met the songwriter Irving Caesar.

Caesar arranged a job for Lenny with a music publisher in Tin Pan Alley. Lenny had to note down the jazz improvisations of performers like saxophonist Coleman Hawkins by listening to records and tapes. He was uniquely qualified for this work. No one but Lenny could transcribe onto sheet music the sounds he heard on the record. Lenny also had to make piano arrangements of novelty tunes and write his own pop songs. The chorus of one song he wrote was called "Now I Know" and began, "Now I know where those stars a-light/that fall in the night/keep shining in your eyes so very bright." He felt embarrassed about using his real name, so he chose a pseudonym, Lenny Amber. He was making a joke, said Shirley. "Bernstein in German means 'amberstone.'" But Lenny earned twenty-five dollars a week. "That job at least rescued him from the ultimate defeat of returning to Boston and Sam's business," said Burtie. "He had some money to live on and some time to compose."

Lenny was working on a piece for soprano and orchestra based on the Book of Lamentations. Developed from another piece called "Hebrew Song," he expanded it into *Jeremiah* (Symphony no. 1). Lenny hurried to finish it in time for a competition sponsored by the New England Conservatory of Music, in Boston. Kouss was the chairman of the jury. Lenny felt he had a good chance of winning. The deadline for submitting entries was December 31st. Shirley came to New York from Mount Holyoke College on Christmas vacation to see him and found him frantically working on the manuscript. His eyes were red "from lack of sleep. He was still deep in composing the last of the three movements, [and] the scoring was only half done," she said. There were just three days left till the deadline. Shirley and a group of friends pitched in to help Lenny. Edys Merrill, the girl who shared Lenny's apartment to save money, made coffee for everyone. Since the score had to be submitted anonymously, it was Edys who went to Boston and handed it to Kouss's secretary on New Year's Eve.

Lenny didn't win. "But it won some points with Sam, who relished its Jewish thematic material and its dedication to him," wrote Burtie.

Lenny wrote another piece, a set of five songs for soprano and piano called *Kid Songs*, or *I Hate Music*. The title came from Edys. Their apartment was on the top floor, and Lenny had the front room. Aaron Copland had paid to have a rented Steinway grand hoisted through the window to Lenny's room. As usual Lenny played till all hours, coaching opera singers, rehearsing the Revuers, and doing his piano arrangements. Edys worked at a war plant during the day. At night, she recalled, "I would walk around the apartment with my hands over my ears screaming, 'I hate music—la de da de da.'" Lenny wrote one of the playful songs based on what she screamed—"I hate music! But I like to sing—: la dee da da dee"—and dedicated the piece to her.

A page of the score for "I Hate Music!" handwritten by Lenny.

In February he performed a new piano sonata by Aaron Copland at Town Hall in New York City. Aaron asked him to do this at the last minute, because he couldn't leave California to play the piece himself. Lenny had only one day to practice, but his performance was a "great success," he wrote to Miss Coates. Lukas Foss, his classmate from Curtis and Tanglewood, was in the audience with Lenny's father. Sam turned to Lukas during the applause and said, "It's all very nice to get all this applause and appreciation, but where's the money?"

Lenny was barely scraping by with his "boring jobs," he recalled. "He had no help from home," said Edys. "He was completely on his own." It gave Lenny some satisfaction when a clarinet sonata he had composed was performed in April at a New York Public Library concert. He had developed the piece from a melody Adolph doodled on the piano one day while Lenny was taking a bath. So he called it *Extension of a Theme by Adolph Green*. The music publisher Lenny worked for offered to publish it immediately and doubled his salary, too. Now he was earning fifty dollars a week!

The publisher also wanted to include *Jeremiah* in their catalogue. Encouraged, Lenny sent copies of the score to his two conducting teachers, Kouss and Reiner. Kouss was unenthusiastic, but Reiner called and said he wanted to perform the composition with the Pittsburgh Symphony Orchestra, perhaps with Lenny conducting. "Lovely, lovely news!" wrote Lenny to Aaron. But Reiner wanted Lenny to add a fourth movement to the work, because in its present form it sounded "too sad."

"Same criticism my father had," wrote Lenny, "which raises Pop in my estimation no end." Lenny didn't feel like working on the piece anymore. "I want to get on with something else," he said. He never did add a fourth movement to *Jeremiah*.

In May, according to the archives of the New York Philharmonic, Artur Rodzinski, the newly appointed director of the orchestra, had put Lenny on a short list of possible assistant conductors. He sent Lenny a letter saying, "Please let me know what your plans are for next season and how is your military status?" Lenny wrote back and said that he had been rejected by the draft board. Rodzinski replied, "I am very glad to hear from you that you have been put in Class 4F *[sic]*. This is very good for the future plans." He ended the letter by saying that he and Lenny "would have a nice long talk about it."

Lenny's version of the story went like this: He had no idea that Rodzinski was considering him for the position when he went up to Lenox in August to visit Kouss for a week. That summer there was no festival at Tanglewood. The school had been shut down and concerts suspended because of the war. However, Kouss felt strongly about helping the war effort. "He was also rediscovering himself as a Jew," wrote Lenny. Because of Hitler "many Jewish people who had either denied their Jewishness or forgotten it . . . were suddenly feeling quite Jewish."

Kouss invited Lenny to assist him in a series of lecture-recitals to be held at the Lenox Library for the benefit of the Red Cross. It was the day before Lenny's twenty-fifth birthday, and he felt gloomy. The coming year looked "as bleak" as the past one. "I was at a low point,"

Lenny playing the piano at a benefit for the Red Cross.

he said. "I felt I wasn't any good to my country. I wasn't any good to music. I kept writing music but I didn't have a place in the musical world." Shirley went with him to cheer him up.

The benefit concert on a Saturday night included a recital by a new singer, Jennie Tourel. Lenny brought *I Hate Music* to rehearsals. Koussevitzky didn't like the songs and would not allow them to be on the program. But at the end of her recital, Jennie sang the songs for an encore.

The next day Kouss's wife told Lenny that Rodzinski, who had a farm in nearby Stockbridge, had called and wanted to see him. Lenny took a bus over to Rodzinski's summer home, White Goat Farm. Rodzinski, born in Poland and trained in Vienna, had come to the United States and had taught conducting at Curtis before Reiner. He had also run the Cleveland Orchestra for many years. During the summer he enjoyed farming as a hobby. He kept herds of goats and cows and also tended bees. When he met Lenny at the entrance of the farm, Rodzinski was wearing shorts and a beekeeper's hat. They sat down on a haystack and talked. It was then, according to Lenny, that Rodzinski told him that he was about to take over as music director of the New York Philharmonic and needed an assistant conductor. "I have been through all the young conductors that I know of in my mind," said Rodzinski, "and I finally asked God whom shall I take and God said, 'Take Bernstein.'"

Lenny said, "I freaked out, I mean, you know, God! . . . I don't know how Rodzinski had managed to find access to this extraordinary

Lenny with Artur Rodzinski, Stockbridge, Massachusetts, 1943.

recommender but I didn't ask. I just said, 'Yes, of course!' I was happy as a bird. . . . My whole life had changed suddenly on my birthday, on that remarkable coincidental birthday, the twenty-fifth birthday on the twenty-fifth of August. I was suddenly going to get a real salary, live in a real place in Carnegie Hall and have a real job."

14

Suddenly Famous

After celebrating with his family in Sharon, Lenny went to New York. He met Bruno Zirato, assistant director of the New York Philharmonic, who arranged for him to rent a one-room apartment in Carnegie Hall. Now Lenny was earning $125 a week! Sam lost almost all hope that Lenny would work for the Samuel Bernstein Hair Company, but he thought maybe Lenny would move back to Boston if he got tired of his duties.

As assistant conductor, Lenny had to study the scores for the week's concert, attend rehearsals, check sound levels in Carnegie Hall, and run errands. When his parents once asked him if he would ever have a chance to conduct a performance of the New York Philharmonic, he told them "not to hold their breath," recalled Burtie. In the

Jennie Tourel.

memory of the New York Philharmonic, remembered Lenny, "no conductor had ever gotten sick" and made it necessary for an assistant to step in. And in those days "no one ever conducted an orchestra unless he was at least in his forties and even then he was considered very young." What's more, Lenny was Jewish and American, doubly rare in the world of classical music.

In the fall Lenny's new friend Jennie Tourel planned to make her New York debut at Town Hall. She chose *I Hate Music* as part of her program and asked Lenny to accompany her again on the piano. He was "wildly excited" that his composition would be performed for a New York audience and "demanded the family's presence." Shirley was away at college and couldn't come, but Sam, Jennie, and Burtie, age eleven, took the train down from Boston. "Sam rushed us through dinner so that we would be at Town Hall at least an hour before the recital began," remembered Burtie. Lenny met them in the lobby and gave them their tickets. "My brother seemed unusually atremble," recalled Burtie. What Lenny didn't tell them was that earlier in the day he had received a phone call saying that Bruno Walter, the guest conductor of the Philharmonic for seven concerts, had become sick and might not be able to conduct the next day. And if Rodzinski couldn't drive down from "snowbound Stockbridge," where there had been a sudden storm, Lenny would have to take over.

The Jennie Tourel concert that night, November 13, 1943, was a great success. The audience particularly enjoyed *I Hate Music*. "I was thrilled," said Lenny. Afterward Jennie gave a party in her apartment.

She sang Russian folk songs, and Lenny played blues and boogie-woogie improvisations. Sam felt "uncomfortable among all those 'artist people'," said Burtie, and he whisked Burtie and *his* Jennie back to the hotel.

Lenny stayed at the party, playing the piano till dawn, and returned to his apartment for a few hours of sleep. At nine o'clock he was awakened by a phone call from Bruno Zirato, the assistant director of the Philharmonic. Bruno Walter was too sick to perform, and Rodzinski was stranded by the snowstorm. "You have to conduct at three o'clock this afternoon," said Zirato to Lenny. Furthermore, the sold-out concert was going to be broadcast nationwide over the radio. "I was scared out of my wits," remembered Lenny. "There was no time for me to rehearse." Lenny dashed over to the hotel where Bruno Walter was staying, and they spent an hour going over the scores.

Then Lenny called the hotel where his family was staying. They were about to leave for Boston, but he told them to book their rooms for another night and go over to Carnegie Hall to pick up their tickets. "He, Lenny Bernstein, was going to conduct the Philharmonic that very afternoon," recalled Burtie.

"*Oy, gevalt!*" cried his parents, almost in unison, in a mixture of amazement and delight. "Wish me luck," said Lenny. "And come backstage at intermission."

Burtie remembers that his parents called Shirley at Mount Holyoke, along with a few close friends, and told them to listen to the concert on the radio that afternoon. Then they rushed over to Carnegie Hall.

At two o'clock an usher showed them to their seats, in the conductor's box. Burtie was awed by the "majesty and immensity of the place." Jennie kept warning him not to lean too far over the velvet railing. "As the audience filed in," recalled Burtie, "it dawned on me that they were all coming to see my brother, whether they knew it then or not."

The members of the orchestra came onstage and tuned their instruments. Then Bruno Zirato walked out and announced to the audience that they would not hear Bruno Walter that day. There were groans. But instead, he said, they were about "to witness the debut of a full-fledged conductor who was born, educated, and trained in this country."

"He meant my brother," said Burtie.

Then Lenny came out onstage. He looked younger and less elegant than the players. Since he didn't own a "cutaway," the formal daytime coat with tails that conductors usually wore for afternoon concerts, he had put on his "only presentable suit, a double-breasted dark gray sharkskin."

"He sort of hopped onto the podium," remembered Burtie, who joined in the mild applause. "I don't remember much about the music itself, except that it sounded all right to me and that Lenny seemed to know what he was doing."

The first piece was Schumann's *Manfred Overture*. Lenny said, "I remember giving the upbeat. . . . [I]t's a very tricky piece to begin . . . I've heard it several times beginning in a very messy way. But they [the orchestra] came in like angels. . . . [A]nd that's it. . . . It was all a dream."

"With those first three chords sounding full and strong and precise," said Shirley, "his nerves steadied almost immediately."

At intermission Burtie and his parents went backstage to the greenroom filled with reporters, photographers, and "a lot of important-looking people." Lenny hugged Sam and Jennie. "Their eyes were glazed with wonder and emotion," said Burtie. Lenny ruffled his brother's hair and gave him a hug and kiss. "Hey, kid, how did it go?" he said. Burtie was too shy to answer. "But I was proud," he said.

During the second part of the concert, Lenny conducted Strauss's *Don Quixote* and the prelude to Wagner's *Die Meistersinger*. Burtie knew the Wagner themes by heart "from Lenny banging them out on the piano at home." Lenny conducted with his hands, his shoulders, his head. He closed his eyes dreamily at slow passages. Crouched. Bounced. Braced himself for the finish, legs planted far apart. Then he opened his arms wide as though embracing the whole orchestra. "The orchestra was really with me," he recalled, "giving me everything it had, all their attention." His upraised fist trembled as the last notes were played.

"There was a moment of silence," remembered Shirley, who was listening on the radio, "then a roar of applause."

"The house roared like one giant animal in the zoo," said Burtie. "It was certainly the loudest human sound I had ever heard—thrilling and eerie. People were shouting at Lenny and the orchestra. Some of

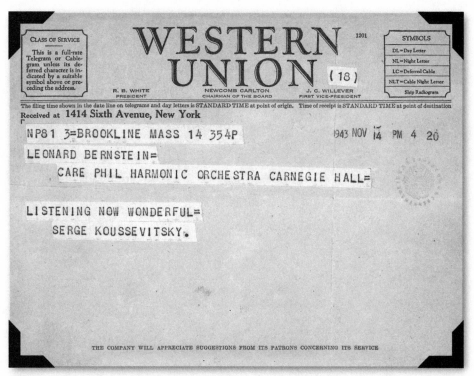

Telegram from Koussevitsky to Lenny during the concert.

them moved toward the front of the stage." Even the orchestra "stood up and cheered," remembered the violinist who played that day. "You just couldn't believe a young man could create that kind of music." Lenny took bow after bow, smiling radiantly. "Once he waved to us in the box," said Burtie, "and everybody stared."

Backstage in the greenroom a crush of people surrounded Lenny. A path was cleared for Sam, Jennie, and Burtie. They hugged and kissed Lenny. Lenny recalled that his father stood there "absolutely dazzled, bewildered, stupefied because he had seen thousands of

Lenny backstage with members of the New York Philharmonic following his debut, November 14, 1943.

people . . . on their feet screaming and cheering for his little Lenny who had been standing there conducting all afternoon. And he really realized it was all possible. And there was a great moment of forgiveness and very deep emotion."

Reporters cornered Sam and Jennie and asked for comments. "I'm very proud of him," Jennie kept repeating. But Sam said, "Just the other day I said to Lenny, 'If you could only conduct the *Don Quixote!*' And he said, 'Dad, you'll have to wait ten years for that.'"

Of course, recalled Burtie, Sam had never heard of *Don Quixote* before that afternoon.

The next morning all the New York papers gave Lenny rave reviews. "I couldn't believe it," said Lenny. "Suddenly I was famous." A headline on the front page of the *New York Times* read, "Young aide leads Philharmonic," and the critic used such words as "brilliant" and "exciting." An editorial in the *Times* said, "It's a good American success story." And the Daily News ran a headline, "Boy Conductor Gets His Chance."

Now Sam's clients, owners of beauty salons, wanted to place their orders directly with him so they could talk about his son Lenny. When a reporter asked Sam why he had ever objected to Lenny's desire to be a musician, Sam replied, "How could I know my son was going to grow up to be Leonard Bernstein?"

To the
New York Philharmonic
Symphony Society
in deepest
gratitude & for
giving me my
great opportunity

Sincerely,
Leonard Bernstein

NYC – 2/4/44

Lenny backstage at Carnegie Hall, New York City. Inscribed to the New York Philharmonic Symphony Society and published in the January 1944 issue of Harper's Bazaar.

Epilogue

After Lenny's sensational debut conducting the New York Philharmonic, he went on to have a long and prolific career as a conductor, composer, pianist, writer, and teacher. Although for years his father worried "that it would all come tumbling down," Burtie remembered, Lenny's success kept soaring.

Torn between conducting and composing—and between writing classical music and musical theater—Lenny shifted gears from one interest to another. As a composer of Broadway shows, he is best known for his hits *On the Town*, *West Side Story*, *Candide*, and *Wonderful Town*. His symphonic works include *Jeremiah* (Symphony no. 1), dedicated to his father; *Age of Anxiety*, after W. H. Auden's poem and dedicated to Koussevitzky; and *Fancy Free*, a ballet score. As a conductor

Lenny traveled throughout the world giving concerts with the New York Philharmonic as well as performing as a guest conductor with symphony orchestras in foreign countries.

In his personal life Lenny felt attracted to both men and women and had many romantic relationships. He married Chilean actress Felicia Montealegre in 1951, and they had three children, Jamie, Alexander, and Nina. Perhaps Lenny achieved his greatest fame when he began televising a series of "Young People's Concerts" from Carnegie Hall in New York, from 1958 to 1972. His daughter Jamie often helped him with the scripts. Encouraging children to "hear with new ears," he thought up innovative ways of introducing them to music. Adults also enjoyed the programs, which were recently released on DVD.

Throughout the years Lenny taught and mentored young musicians, especially at Tanglewood, which had been so important to his development as a musician. On August 19, 1990, at Tanglewood, Lenny conducted his last concert with great effort. He had survived a bout of cancer and was suffering from emphysema, a lung disease partly due to smoking, which made it hard for him to breathe. On October 14, 1990, at the age of seventy-two, he died of a heart attack brought on by emphysema and pulmonary infections. But Leonard Bernstein will always live on as one of America's most important and dynamic musical figures. He set the precedent for young Americans to become conductors of major symphony orchestras, a profession traditionally dominated by older Europeans. As his brother, Burton, said, "Lenny made it possible."

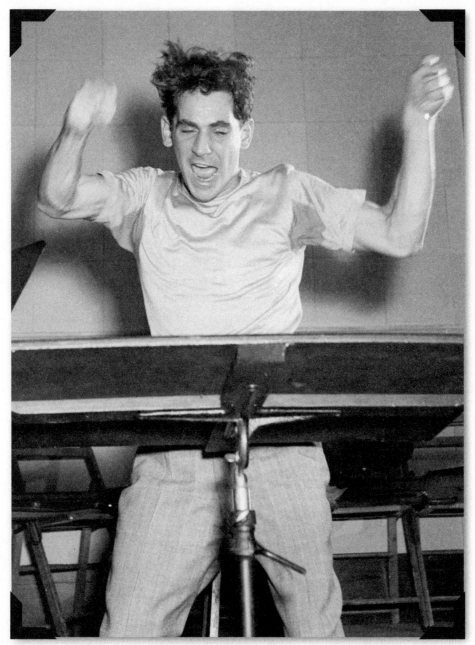

Lenny conducting in rehearsal, Carnegie Hall.

Timeline

1918   August 25, Leonard Bernstein is born in Lawrence, Massachusetts.

1923   October 23, Shirley Bernstein is born. Lenny and Shirley's father opens the Samuel J. Bernstein Hair Company. Lenny receives a piano from his aunt Clara and begins lessons with Frieda Karp.

1930   Lenny starts lessons with Susan Williams.

1931   Lenny has his bar mitzvah. Sam buys him a new piano.

1932   January 31, Burton "Bertie" Bernstein is born. Lenny begins attending Boston Latin School and starts piano lessons with Helen Coates.

1935   Lenny graduates Boston Latin School and enters Harvard College. He starts piano lessons with Heinrich Gebhard.

1937   Lenny meets Dimitri Mitropolous, Adolph Green, and Aaron Copland. October 31, Lenny performs the Ravel Piano Concerto with the State Symphony Orchestra, his first professional appearance as a solo pianist with an orchestra.

1939   Lenny graduates Harvard and moves to New York City. In the fall he enters Curtis Institute in Philadelphia and studies conducting with Fritz Reiner and piano with Isabelle Vengerova. World War II begins.

1940   Serge Koussevitzky opens the Berkshire Music Center and Tanglewood. Lenny is in the first class of students.

1941   Lenny graduates from Curtis. The United States enters World War II.

1942   Lenny moves back to New York and gets a job with a music publisher. He completes *Jeremiah* (Symphony no.1).

1943   August 25, Lenny's 25th birthday, he meets Artur Rodzinski and is appointed the assistant conductor of the New York Philharmonic. November 14, Lenny makes his conducting debut at Carnegie Hall.

1944   *On The Town* premieres on Broadway. First performances of *Jeremiah* and ballet *Fancy Free*.

1947–48 Lenny conducts the Palestine Philharmonic Orchestra, later renamed the Israel Philharmonic Orchestra, during Israel's War of Independence.

1949   First performance of Second Symphony, *Age of Anxiety*, with Koussevitzky conducting and Lenny as solo pianist.

1950   Premiere of *Peter Pan*.

1951   Lenny marries Chilean actress Felicia Montealegre. He is appointed professor of music at Brandeis University in Waltham, Massachusetts.

1952   September 8, daughter Jamie is born. First performance of *Trouble in Tahiti*.

1953   Lenny becomes the first American to conduct at La Scala Opera House in Milan, Italy. Premiere of *Wonderful Town*, New York City.

1954   Lenny's first television appearance on *Omnibus*.

1955   July 7, son Alexander is born.

1956   Premiere of *Candide*, New York City.

1957   Premiere of *West Side Story* on Broadway. Lenny takes to conducting with a baton because of back pain.

1958   Lenny begins his series of Young People's Concerts. He also starts a new television series, *Leonard Bernstein and the New York Philharmonic*, geared for adults.

1959   Lenny's first book, *The Joy of Music*, is published.

1962   February 28, daughter Nina is born.

1963   First performance of Lenny's Third Symphony, *Kaddish*, in Tel Aviv.

1964   Lenny debuts as conductor of the Metropolitan Opera in New York City.

1966   Lenny's book *The Infinite Variety of Music* is published.

1968   Lenny leads celebrations of the New York Philharmonic's 125th anniversary.

1969   April 30, Samuel Bernstein dies. Lenny retires from the New York Philharmonic Orchestra and is named conductor laureate.

1970   Lenny becomes an advisor to Tanglewood.

1971   Lenny conducts his 1,000th concert with the New York Philharmonic, the first conductor ever to do so.

1972   Lenny conducts *Carmen* at the Metropolitan Opera House, New York City.

1973   Lenny delivers the Charles Eliot Norton lectures at Harvard. He separates from his wife, Felicia.

1977   Lenny reconciles with Felicia.

1978   June 16, Felicia dies.

1980   November 14, Lenny conducts Aaron Copland's *Lincoln Portrait*, with Copland as narrator, on the composer's 80th birthday.

1982   Lenny's book *Findings* is published.

1990   August 19, Lenny conducts his last concert at Tanglewood. October 14, Lenny dies at his New York home.

Biographies

Helen Coates

Soon after Lenny's extraordinary debut at Carnegie Hall, he was besieged with offers and fan mail and needed a secretary. At first his sister, Shirley, handled the responsibility. Then in 1944 Lenny asked his former piano teacher, Helen Coates, to take over. She was so devoted to Lenny that she didn't tell him she couldn't type, and she hired someone else to do that part of the job. Miss Coates remained Lenny's loyal assistant, friend, and confidante for decades until her retirement.

Betty Comden

Lenny met Betty Comden in 1939 when he accompanied the Revuers. She liked him right away and remembered him as "full of enthusiasm and fun." By the time Betty and Adolph created *On the Town* with Lenny, they were an established writing team. Besides co-writing *On the Town*, Betty performed a starring role in the show, and so did Adolph. Betty, born Elizabeth Cohen in Brooklyn in 1917, studied drama at New York University, graduated in 1938, and changed her last name to Comden. When she joined the Washington Square Players, Betty met Adolph. Their professional partnership began when they formed the Revuers. They met daily (usually in Betty's living room) to work on a project or just talk "to keep up a continuity of working," she said. In addition to their many awards, they were both elected to the Theater Hall of Fame and the Songwriters Hall of Fame. Throughout the years Betty, Adolph, and their families remained close friends with Lenny and his family. Betty visited Lenny at his bedside the day before he died, and they laughed together recalling a Revuers' number about famous movie villains of the 1930s. In 2006 Betty died of heart failure at the age of eighty-nine. She will always be remembered for her witty shows and songs.

Aaron Copland

Lenny met Aaron Copland on November 14, 1937. It was Copland's thirty-seventh birthday, and he was already established as a modern American composer. Born in Brooklyn, New York, in 1900 to parents who were Jewish immigrants from Russia, Copland began studying piano as a boy. After graduating from high school, he continued studying music instead of going to college, and in 1921 he earned a scholarship to attend a summer school for American musicians in France.

Copland stayed in Paris for three years. Back in the United States, he created a new kind of American music inspired by folk songs, hymns, and blues rhythms. His most famous works include the ballet scores *Rodeo*, *Billy the Kid*, and *Appalachian Spring*, which is based on a Shaker melody. A beloved teacher and lecturer, Copland helped many young musicians like Lenny. Lenny in turn championed Copland's music in the concert hall, and they remained lifelong friends. Copland died on December 2, 1990, just months after Lenny's death.

Lukas Foss

Lukas Foss was one of the child prodigies Lenny met at Curtis Institute. Lenny described him as an "authentic genius." Born in Berlin, Germany, in 1922, Lukas began studying piano and theory as a child, and at age seven wrote his first composition for piano. At age eleven Lukas and his family fled to Paris to escape the Nazis, and in 1937 they emigrated to the United States and settled in New York City. "He slept under the piano, because there wasn't room for a bed in the apartment," later recalled his wife, Cornelia Brendel Foss.

Inspired by Aaron Copland's modern American music, Lukas composed *The Prairie*, based on a poem by Carl Sandburg. The work had its premiere at Town Hall in New York when Lukas was just twenty-two. He went on to achieve fame and win honors not only as a composer but also as a conductor, pianist, and professor. In 1961 Lenny conducted the premiere of Lukas's *Time Cycle*, and that same year

Lukas conducted the premiere of Lenny's Symphonic Dances from *West Side Story*. During the summers they both worked with young musicians at Tanglewood. In August 1990, when Lenny was seriously ill, Lukas asked him how he was doing during a rehearsal break. "I'm still upright," said Lenny. Lukas said jokingly, "You're better than a piano: you're both upright and grand." Two months later Lenny died, and Lukas was one of the many friends attending the funeral. At age eighty-six Lukas was still composing and set a poem by his son, Christopher Foss, to music. Lukas died on February 1, 2009. He was eighty-seven.

Adolph Green

Lenny met Adolph Green at Camp Onota in 1937, when they put on a performance of *The Pirates of Penzance*. Lenny was nineteen; Adolph was twenty-three and trying to establish a career as a composer and performer. They became good friends despite the fact that Lenny's father couldn't stand Adolph and called him "a crazy artist nut." Adolph, born in 1914 in the Bronx, attended City College of New York and, while a student, began acting with the Washington Square Players. In the late 1930s he got together with four other performers, including Betty Comden and Judy Holliday, and formed a group called the Revuers that put on musical comedy skits at the Village Vanguard nightclub in New York. The Revuers couldn't afford to pay royalties on previously written material, so Adolph and Betty wrote their own songs and routines. In 1939 Lenny spent the summer with Adolph, and he often accompanied the Revuers on the piano. Their friendship developed into a professional collaboration. In 1944 Lenny expanded his ballet score *Fancy Free*, composed for dancer and choreographer Jerome Robbins, into a Broadway musical, *On the Town*. Lenny asked Betty and Adolph to write the book (the text of a musical) and lyrics. The show was a smash and was later adapted as a movie. Comden and Green, as they were known, created one hit after another for stage and screen. Their film *Singin' in the Rain* is considered one of the best American movies ever made. Adolph and Betty's professional partnership lasted for sixty years, the longest-running creative partnership in the history of theater. Adolph died in October 2002, and two months later Broadway turned out in full force for a memorial program.

Serge Koussevitzky

Lenny began a close relationship with his teacher Serge Koussevitzky at Tanglewood in 1940 and later said that Kouss, as he called him, remained one of the strongest influences in his life. Koussevitzky was born in Russia in 1874. At age fourteen he ran away from home to study music at the School of the Moscow Philharmonic and became a virtuoso bassist. He married the daughter of a rich tea merchant, and they moved to Berlin, where he pursued his goal of becoming a conductor. Upon returning to Russia he founded his own orchestra. But with the outbreak of the Bolshevik Revolution, he and his wife fled to Paris. There he became acquainted with Aaron Copland. When the Boston Symphony Orchestra invited Koussevitzky to become its music director, he readily accepted, and he asked Copland to compose a symphony for the coming season. During the twenty-five years that Koussevitzky directed the Boston Symphony Orchestra, he always featured modern music by contemporary composers, such as Samuel Barber, George Gershwin, and Aaron Copland, to acquaint audiences with new American sounds. In 1940 he established the Berkshire (now Tanglewood) Music Center as a place to train promising young musicians. Lenny was one of his first students. Kouss died on June 4, 1951. When Lenny got married a couple of months later, he wore a suit and pair of shoes that had belonged to Kouss, and whenever he conducted he wore a pair of Kouss's cuff links and kissed them for luck before going onstage.

Dimitri Mitropoulos

While Lenny was a student at Harvard, he heard Dimitri Mitropoulos conduct for the first time.

Mitropoulos, born in a village in Greece in 1896, was musically precocious, like Lenny, and began composing at an early age. He studied music at the Athens Conservatoire, as well as in Brussels and Berlin. At a 1930 concert with the Berlin Philharmonic, he achieved sudden fame when he played the Prokofiev Third Piano Concerto and conducted from the keyboard, one of the first modern musicians to do so. In 1936, and again the following year, Koussevitzky invited him to be guest conductor of the Boston Symphony Orchestra. Mitropoulos had a vigorous, passionate conducting style that greatly influenced Lenny. He was physically powerful and loved mountain climbing. A deeply religious man, Mitropoulos always wore a silver Greek cross with a dove carved on it.

After serving as conductor of the Minneapolis Symphony Orchestra from 1937 to 1949, Mitropoulos went on to conduct the New York Philharmonic from 1949 to 1958. In the 1957–1958 season he shared the post with Lenny. Then Mitropoulos announced he was leaving to devote more time to opera, and Lenny would succeed him. In 1960 Mitropoulos died while conducting a rehearsal of Gustav Mahler's Third Symphony at La Scala Opera House in Milan, Italy. A friend of one of Lenny's composer friends was there and retrieved Mitropoulos's Greek cross. He passed it on to Lenny, who treasured it as a good-luck charm.

Sid Ramin

Sid's first piano teacher was Lenny. The lessons started when Sid was twelve and continued while Lenny was at Harvard. Sid went on to study music at the New England Conservatory, then orchestration at Columbia University in New York City. "Orchestration," said Sid, "means deciding which instrument will play what—violin? Trumpet? Or in combinations." He was working on a weekly television show when Lenny called him and asked him to orchestrate *West Side Story*. Sid didn't have time to tackle the project alone, so he asked a colleague, Irwin Kostal, to do it with him, and they finished in a month. Later Sid scored the music for the movie adaptation of *West Side Story* and won an Oscar. Through the years Sid continued to work closely with Lenny as well as with other famed composers of Broadway musicals. He also wrote movie scores and award-winning advertising jingles. Sid and Lenny always kept their childhood language, Rybernian, a secret. Sometimes Sid would see Lenny backstage after a concert and whisper the password. "In the midst of everything," said Sid, Lenny would "fall on the floor" laughing. Today Sid serves as artistic advisor to the Leonard Bernstein estate. From time to time he is asked to orchestrate a piece that Lenny composed for a soloist or very small combination of instruments. At age eighty-seven Sid said, "I don't think a day goes by that I don't think about Lenny in some way. . . . If it sounds like worshipping somebody, so be it. That's the way it was."

Fritz Reiner

Lenny encountered Fritz Reiner when he auditioned for his conducting class at the Curtis Institute. Reiner, born in Budapest, Hungary, in 1888, had studied piano and composition at the Franz Liszt Academy. His piano teacher was composer Béla Bartók. After engagements at opera houses in Budapest, Hungary, and Dresden, Germany, Reiner came to the United States at age thirty-three to take over the Cincinnati Symphony. He was known for setting "impossibly high standards," said Lenny, and losing his temper daily. During rehearsals of the Cincinnati Symphony Orchestra, he would single out a player and ask where he had studied. On being told, Reiner would answer, "You were cheated! You should get your money back!" Within three years only twenty-seven musicians were left of an orchestra of ninety-two. Reiner began to teach at the Curtis Institute in 1931 and conducted the Pittsburgh Symphony Orchestra from 1938 to 1948. Again, he terrorized the musicians, and half of them quit each season. Nevertheless, he was considered a great conductor. In 1953 he became music director of the Chicago Symphony Orchestra, and the recordings he made during this period are considered his finest. His conducting technique consisted of small gestures, indicating the beat by the tip of his baton. In later years Lenny praised Reiner as the "supreme master of the baton," who taught him that "every movement must be concentrated on getting the orchestra to produce the sound you think the composer wanted."

Ultimately, Lenny and Reiner became "very good friends." On November 2, 1963, Lenny titled his televised Young People's Concert "A Tribute to Teachers" and honored Reiner among the musicians who had educated him. A couple of weeks later, on November 15, 1963, Reiner died just before his seventy-fifth birthday.

Harold Shapero

Harold Shapero, two years younger than Lenny, lived a couple of blocks away in Newton but didn't meet him until they were students at Harvard. Shapero was mainly interested in composition and had written an early woodwind trio during his freshman year. His teacher thought it was pretty good and mailed it to Aaron Copland. Copland liked it and said, "You don't expect to get anything good in the mail!" He then sent a postcard to Lenny, whom he had recently met, and wrote, "Look to your laurels in your neighborhood, there may be another composer." Lenny immediately marched over to Shapero's house to see the piece. He deemed it "lousy," but they became friends. At Harvard they took a seminar together, shopped for records at Briggs and Briggs, and were roommates at Tanglewood in the first season, 1940.

They realized that they were both skilled pianists and decided to perform duets to earn money. While at Harvard they played locally and sometimes took a train to New York City when they had a job. Once Shapero composed a piece for them to play, Four-Hand Sonata for Piano, and dedicated it to Lenny and himself.

After graduating from Harvard in 1941, Shapero continued studying piano and composition. In 1947 he composed Symphony for Classical Orchestra. Lenny conducted the world premiere with the Boston Symphony Orchestra and made one of the first recordings of the piece. In 1951 Shapero was hired to start a music department at Brandeis University. He stayed until his retirement, in 1988, when he decided to devote himself to composition. Now, at age eighty-eight, he is still working.

Mildred Spiegel Zucker

Lenny and Mildred met when they were high school students. "We quickly became musical friends," she recalled. "He'd bounce up the stairs, run into the kitchen, give my mother a bear hug and lift the pot covers to see what was cooking," she said. Then he would "run into the living room, pound on my new Baldwin Grand Piano, and a few times broke the strings, which the tuner had to replace."

Mildred was the official pianist of the Boston Public School Senior Symphony. In 1933, at age seventeen, she played the Beethoven First Piano Concerto in public. Before the performance Lenny rehearsed the orchestral part with her. Years later when he conducted and played the concerto with the Boston Symphony Orchestra, he told everyone that he "learned it from Mildred."

When he was in college, Leonard composed a piece for Mildred, *Music for the Dance*, in honor of her twenty-first birthday. He signed it, "With all my heart, Leonard Bernstein, June 12, 1937." "He also wrote a piano trio for my Madison Trio," she remembered, "which we played at Harvard."

Mildred became a teacher, married, and moved to New York, but she stayed in touch with Lenny. "Lenny sent eighty-four letters and postcards to me over the years," she said. "Only Aaron Copland received as many letters from him." At the end of a memoir she wrote about their friendship, Mildred wrote, "There never was and never will be another Lenny."

Lenny's Music

Reading about Leonard Bernstein is incomplete without listening to his music: the jazzy, joyous rhythms of "Three Dance Episodes" from *On the Town* or the ballet *Fancy Free*, which makes you want to jump in the air and dance, or the stirring overture to *Candide*, Lenny's opera adapted from the novella by Voltaire. The opening lines of the opera sung by the young hero, *Candide*, perhaps best express Lenny's musical spirit:

> *Life is happiness indeed:*
> *Mares to ride and books to read.*
> *Though of noble birth I'm not,*
> *I'm delighted with my lot.*

Knowing Lenny is impossible without hearing him on a recording passionately conduct *El Salon Mexico*, composed by his friend and mentor, Aaron Copland, or a Mahler symphony, or Beethoven's Ninth. But understanding Lenny's musical life also requires enjoying his most famous songs from *West Side Story*: "Jet Song," "America," "Tonight," and the haunting "Somewhere."

Then there's Lenny talking about music on his televised concerts for young people, with themes such as "The World of Jazz," "Introduction to Modern Music," and "The Art of Conducting." In these

151

concerts you can feel his excitement as he runs to the piano to demon-strate a point. In an article for a dance magazine, Lenny once wrote about the fun in music. He talked about music as "a series of notes, arranged in certain orders and patterns that . . . have the power to pro-duce a substantial effect on us." He discussed the fun composers have in creating these works. The article ended with Lenny's advice: "We ab-stract artists, we musicians and dancers, have this to say to ourselves: Relax. Invent. Perform. Have fun."

So as Lenny would say, "Have fun," and experience the joy of his music.

Discography

Leonard Bernstein was one of the most recorded conductors in history. A complete list of all his recordings of works by other composers and those of his own works would be too long to include here. The fol-lowing are some of the CDs I think readers would particularly enjoy, and the ones from my collection that I listened to over and over as I worked on this book.

From the author's collection

Leonard Bernstein, *Candide*. London Symphony Orchestra and Chorus, Leonard Bernstein, conductor. Deutsche Grammophon, 1991. (This recording features Adolph Green as one of the singers.)

Bernstein Conducts Bernstein: *Fancy Free, Facsimile, On the Town: 3 Dance Episodes*. Israel Philharmonic Orchestra. Deutsche Grammophon, 1979.

Discography

Bernstein Conducts Bernstein: *Jeremiah* (Symphony No. 1), *The Age of Anxiety* (Symphony No.2), *I Hate Music!*, *La Bonne Cuisine*. Jennie Tourel, mezzo-soprano, Leonard Bernstein, piano. Sony, 1999.

Copland, Aaron. *Billy the Kid, Rodeo*. New York Philharmonic, Leonard Bernstein, conductor. CBS Records, 1981.

Ravel, Maurice. *Bolero, La Valse, Alborada Del Gradioso, Daphnis et Chloe* Suite No. 2. New York Philharmonic, Leonard Bernstein, conductor. CBS Records, 1981.

Stravinsky, Igor. *Symphony of Psalms*, Concerto for Piano and Wind Instruments, *Pulcinella Suite*. London Symphony Orchestra and New York Philharmonic, Leonard Bernstein, conductor; Seymour Lipkin, piano. Sony, 1977.

A partial list of recordings of works by other composers with Leonard Bernstein, conductor. Many of these pieces are mentioned in the text.

Brahms, Johannes. *Academic Festival Overture*, Op. 83. New York Philharmonic. Manhattan Center, New York. Sony, 1993.

Britten, Benjamin. *Young People's Guide to the Orchestra*, Op. 34. New York Philharmonic, Henry Chapin, narrator. Sony, 1961.

———. (in Hebrew) New York Philharmonic, Isaac Shimony, narrator. Manhattan Center, New York. Sony, 1961.

———. (in Spanish) New York Philharmonic, Felicia Montealegre (Leonard Bernstein's wife), narrator. Sony, 1961.

Copland, Aaron. *El Salon Mexico*; Concerto for Clarinet and String Orchestra. Deutsche Grammophon, 1991.

———. Concerto for Piano and Orchestra, New York Philharmonic, Aaron Copland, piano. Philharmonic Hall, New York. Sony, 1964.

———. *Appalachian Spring*. New York Philharmonic. Sony, 1961.

Gershwin, George. *Rhapsody in Blue*. Columbia Symphony Orchestra, Leonard Bernstein, piano and conductor. Sony, 1959.

———. Prelude for Piano. Los Angeles Philharmonic Orchestra, Leonard Bernstein, piano and conductor. Deutsche Grammophon, 1982.

———. *An American in Paris*. New York Philharmonic. Sony, 1958.

Mendelssohn, Felix. *Hebrides Overture*, Op.26 ("Fingal's Cave"). New York Philharmonic. Sony, 1961.

Mozart, Wolfgang Amadeus. Concerto No. 25 in C Major for Piano and Orchestra, K 503. Israel Philharmonic Orchestra, Leonard Bernstein, piano and conductor. Tel Aviv: Sony, 1974.

Prokofiev, Sergei. *Peter and the Wolf*, Op. 67. New York Philharmonic, Leonard Bernstein, narrator. Saint George Hotel, Brooklyn, New York. Sony, 1960.

Rachmaninoff, Sergei. Concerto N. 2 in C Minor for Piano and Orchestra, Op. 18. Phillipe Entremont, piano. Saint George Hotel, Brooklyn, New York. Sony, 1960.

Ravel, Maurice. Piano Concerto in G Major for Piano and Orchestra. New York Philharmonic Orchestra, Leonard Bernstein, piano and conductor. RCA Victor, 1946.

Rimsky-Korsakov, Nikolai. *Scheherezade*, Op. 35. New York Philharmonic, John Corigliano, violin. Saint George Hotel, Brooklyn, New York. Sony, 1959.

Schuman, William. *American Festival Overture*. Los Angeles Philharmonic Orchestra. San Francisco, Davies Symphony Hall. Deutsche Grammophon, 1982.

Shapero, Harold. Symphony for Classical Orchestra. Columbia Symphony Orchestra. 30th Street Studio, New York. Sony, 1953.

Thompson, Randall. Symphony No. 2 in E Minor. New York Philharmonic. Sony, 1968.

Vaughan Williams, Ralph. *Serenade to Music*. New York Philharmonic. Sony, 1962.

Vivaldi, Antonio. *The Four Seasons*. New York Philharmonic, John Corigliano, violin. Manhattan Center, New York. Sony, 1964.

Bernstein Conducts Bernstein

On the Town (original cast), with Randel Striboneen, a.k.a. Leonard Bernstein, as Bimmy. 30th Street Studio, New York. Sony, 1960.

Symphonic Dances from *West Side Story*, Los Angeles Philharmonic Orchestra. Davies Hall, San Francisco. Deutsche Grammophon, 1982.

Videography

A complete set of the Young People's Concerts on DVD, Kultur D1503, includes the following: *What Is Impressionism?*; *The Latin American Spirit*; *Jazz in the Concert Hall*; *A Tribute to Sibelius*; *The Sound of an Orchestra*; *What Does Music Mean?*; *What is Classical Music?*; *What is American Music?*; *Folk Music in the Concert Hall*; *Humor in Music*; *What is American Music?*

Leonard Bernstein: The Concert Collection, 9-DVD Set, includes the Ravel Concerts, Berlioz Requiem, Verdi Requiem, Beethoven, the Ninth Symphony in D Minor, and *Trouble in Tahiti: An Opera in Seven Scenes* by Leonard Bernstein.

Bibliography

(*) denotes material suitable for younger readers

Books and Articles

Bernstein, Burton. *Family Matters: Sam, Jennie, and the Kids.* Lincoln, NE: An Authors Guild Backinprint.com Edition, 2000.

Bernstein, Leonard. *Findings: Fifty Years of Meditations on Music.* New York: Anchor Books/Doubleday, 1982.

——. "My Teacher, Heinrich Gebhard." In Gebhard, Heinrich. *The Art of Pedaling.* New York: F. Colombo, 1963. Reprinted in Mintz, *My Friend Lenny.*

——. *The Infinite Variety of Music.* New York: Simon and Schuster, 1966.

——. *The Joy of Music.* New York: Simon and Schuster, 1959.

*Bernstein, Shirley. *Making Music: Leonard Bernstein.* Chicago: Encyclopaedia Britannica Press, 1963.

*Blashfield, Jean F. *Leonard Bernstein: Composer and Conductor.* Chicago: Ferguson Publishing Company, 2000.

Briggs, John. *Leonard Bernstein: The Man, His Work, and His World.* Cleveland: World Publishing, 1961.

Burton, Humphrey. *Leonard Bernstein.* New York: Doubleday, 1994.

Copland, Aaron and Vivian Perlis. *Copland: 1900 Through 1942.* New York: St. Martin's Press/Marek, 1984.

Gruen, John. Photographs by Ken Heyman. *The Private World of Leonard Bernstein.* New York: Viking Press, 1968.

Horowitz, Joseph. *Classical Music in America: A History of Its Rise and Fall.* New York: W. W. Norton and Company, 2005.

*Hurwitz, Johanna. *Leonard Bernstein: A Passion for Music.* Philadelphia: Jewish Publication Society, 1993.

*Lazo, Caroline Evensen. *Leonard Bernstein: In Love with Music.* Minneapolis: Lerner Publications Company, 2003.

Mintz, Ouida Blatt. *My Friend Lenny: A Memoir of My Life in Music.* Roslyn Heights, NY: Bravura Books, 2000.

Peyser, Joan. *Bernstein: A Biography*. New York: Billboard Books, an imprint of Watson-Guptill, 1998.

Pollack, Howard. *Aaron Copland: The Life and Work of an Uncommon Man*. New York: Henry Holt and Company, 1999.

Secrest, Meryle. *Leonard Bernstein: A Life*. New York: Alfred A. Knopf, 1994.

Swan, Claudia, editor. *Leonard Bernstein: The Harvard Years 1935–1939*. The Eos Orchestra, New York: The Eos Orchestra, 1999.

*Venezia, Mike. *Leonard Bernstein*. New York: Children's Press, 1997.

Zucker, Mildred Spiegel. "Lenny and Mildred." In Mintz, *My Friend Lenny*.

Exhibits and Multimedia

Audio sessions recorded at *Leonard Bernstein: Boston to Broadway: Concerts and Symposia at Harvard University*, October 12-14, 2006.

Leonard Bernstein: Boston to Broadway: Concerts and Symposia at Harvard University, October 12-14, 2006.

"Leonard Bernstein's Boston Years: Team Research in a Harvard Classroom," http://my.harvard.edu/icb/icb.do?keyword=bernstein

Leonard Bernstein Collection, Music Division, Library of Congress.

Source interviews for *Reflections*, a film taped and recorded at Carnegie Hall by Peter Rosen Productions for the United States Information Agency, 1978. Used by permission of the Leonard Bernstein Office.

Source interviews with Humphrey Burton. Used by permission of the Leonard Bernstein Office.

Interviews conducted by the author in person

Jamie and Alexander Bernstein, March 29, 2007.

Craig Urquhart, March 29, 2007.

Interviews conducted by the author via telephone

Burton Bernstein, April 18, 2007.

Sid Ramin, August 22, 2007, and January 14, 2008.

Letters to the author

Sid Ramin, September 1, 2007, and September 5, 2007.

Sources of Quotations

Page 1: "Moynik!" Leonard Bernstein quoted in Humphrey Burton, *Leonard Bernstein*, p. 7.

Page 3: "Every time . . . to breathe." Jennie Bernstein quoted in Burton Bernstein, *Family Matters*, p. 107.

Page 3: "Oh by Jingo . . . girl for me." Jennie Bernstein quoted in Burton, p. 7.

Page 3: "windowsill pianist" Jennie Bernstein quoted in Ibid., p. 8.

Page 4: "ancient tunes . . . choral music." Leonard Bernstein quoted in Ibid., pp. 8–9.

Page 4: "Arrangement is . . . an opera." Leonard Bernstein quoted in Ibid., p. 9.

Page 5: "first real music I heard" Leonard Bernstein quoted in letter written to Solomon G. Braslavsky, *Leonard Bernstein: Boston to Broadway: Concerts and Symposia at Harvard University*, p. 36, research credit: Lily Yeh, Harvard graduate student.

Page 5: "I never forget . . . was a youngster." Leonard Bernstein quoted in Ibid.

Page 6: "It was what . . . coming true." Samuel Bernstein quoted in B. Bernstein, p. 65.

Page 9: "I remember touching . . . be about music." Leonard Bernstein quoted in Burton, p. 10.

Page 10: "fun things . . . singing hours." Leonard Bernstein quoted in Ibid., p. 8.

Page 10: "Mrs. Fitzgerald . . . dozens of songs." Leonard Bernstein quoted in Ibid., p. 8.

Page 10: "I was safe . . . me feel supreme." Leonard Bernstein quoted in John Gruen, *The Private World of Leonard Bernstein*, p. 39.

Page 10: "'Goodnight Sweetheart.' I knew it had to have . . . and triumphantly." Leonard Bernstein quoted in Burton, p. 11.

Page 10: "Stop that . . . can't sleep." Leonard Bernstein quoted in Ibid., p. 11.

Page 10: "But I . . . in heaven." Leonard Bernstein quoted in Ibid., p. 11.

Page 10: "demanded . . . I knew that." Leonard Bernstein quoted in transcript of oral interview with Humphrey Burton for Burton, *Leonard Bernstein*, Roll #1, p. 13.

Page 11: "After a couple . . . harder stuff." Leonard Bernstein quoted in Burton, p. 11.

Page 11: "This boy is . . . him anymore." Frieda Karp quoted in Ibid., p. 12.

Page 11: "On my own . . . fights began." Leonard Bernstein quoted in B. Bernstein, p. 112–113.

Page 11: "You get one . . . that is it." Leonard Bernstein quoted in transcript of source interviews for *Reflections*, Roll #3, p. 8.

Page 11: "scary dedication" Burton Bernstein quoted in B. Bernstein, p. 113.

Page 13: "Under no . . . a musician." Burton Bernstein quoted in Ibid., p. 113.

Page 13: "American Jewish boys . . . serious music." Burton Bernstein quoted in Ibid., p. 113.

Page 13: "Lenny always played . . . into the night." Jennie Bernstein quoted in Joan Peyser, *Bernstein: A Biography*, p. 24.

Page 14: "Mind if I try?" Sid Ramin quoted in Burton, p. 14.

Page 14: "You're the fellow . . . be teaching." Sid Ramin quoted in Ibid., p. 14.

Page 14: "We would sit down . . . me stuff." Sid Ramin, author's interview, August 22, 2007.

Page 14: "We were inseparable." Sid Ramin, "Leonard Bernstein's Boston Years: Team Research in a Harvard Classroom," interviewed February 21, 2006, research credit: Emily Abrams Ansari, Ryan Bañagale, and Corinna Campbell, Harvard graduate students.

Page 14: "We bought . . . till dawn." Leonard Bernstein quoted in H. Burton interview, Roll #5, p. 13.

Page 14: "I was there . . . sight reader." Sid Ramin, "Leonard Bernstein's Boston Years: Team Research in a Harvard Classroom," interviewed February 21, 2006, research credit: Emily Abrams Ansari, Ryan Bañagale, and Corinna Campbell, Harvard graduate students.

Page 16: "When the Moon . . . Mountain." B. Bernstein, p. 108.

Page 16: "closed society" Burton Bernstein quoted in Ibid., p. 111.

Page 17: "The more money . . . losing it." Burton Bernstein quoted in B. Bernstein, p. 78.

Page 17: "You know, you . . . be a klezmer." Leonard Bernstein quoted in Ibid., pp. 116–117.

Page 18: "His father . . . making a living." Sid Ramin, "Leonard Bernstein's Boston Years: Team Research in a Harvard Classroom," interviewed February 21, 2006, research credit: Emily Abrams Ansari, Ryan Bañagale, and Corinna Campbell, Harvard graduate students.

Page 18: "He [Sam] was very . . . a success." Sid Ramin, author's interview, August 22, 2007.

Page 19: "prefabricated" Leonard Bernstein, transcript of source interviews for *Reflections*, Roll #3, p. 9.

Page 20: "I have two . . . Would I like to go?" Leonard Bernstein, Ibid., Roll #3, p. 23.

Page 20: "I had never . . . a piano arrangement." Leonard Bernstein quoted in Meryle Secrest, *Leonard Bernstein: A Life*, p. 37.

Page 20: "He thought . . . rebellion against him." Leonard Bernstein quoted in Burton, p. 20.

Page 21: "Why don't . . . my business?" Leonard Bernstein quoted in Ibid., p. 20.

Page 21: "It was a . . . thrilled to pieces." Leonard Bernstein quoted in B. Bernstein, p. 115.

Page 22: "I don't think . . . wasn't very good." Leonard Bernstein quoted in Leonard Bernstein, *Findings*, pp. 179–180.

Page 22: "variations on . . . of it myself." Leonard Bernstein quoted in Ibid., p. 180.

Page 22: "The first night . . . still playing." Samuel Bernstein quoted in Secrest, p. 20.

Sources of Quotations

Page 23, caption: "This place . . . with the piano." Leonard Bernstein Collection, Music Division, Library of Congress.

Page 24: "'How?' she said . . . with the right." Shirley Bernstein quoted in Peyser, p. 27.

Page 24: "The competition . . . other hard pieces." Shirley Bernstein quoted in Gruen, p. 145.

Page 24: "There's enough . . . house already." Jennie Bernstein to Shirley Bernstein, quoted in Burton, p. 21.

Page 24: "It was . . . my lungs out." Shirley Bernstein quoted in Peyser, p. 27.

Page 25: "he'd be all . . . it was fun." Shirley Bernstein quoted in Burton, p. 21.

Page 25: "We just sailed . . . of the night." Shirley Bernstein quoted in S. Bernstein, *Making Music*, p. 22. By courtesy of Encyclopaedia Britannica, Inc., copyright © 1963; used with permission.

Page 25: "Stop that damn . . . office tomorrow." Samuel Bernstein quoted in Secrest, p. 23.

Page 25: "chained to the piano" Jennie Bernstein quoted in S. Bernstein, p. 22.

Page 25: "stayed there until . . . without music." Leonard Bernstein quoted in Secrest, p. 28.

Page 25: "and play any music . . . it for years." Mildred Spiegel Zucker quoted in Peyser, p. 35.

Page 25: "I found him playing . . . like an orchestra." Mildred Spiegel Zucker quoted in "Lenny and Mildred," in Ouida Blatt Mintz, *My Friend Lenny: A Memoir*, p. 74.

Page 26: "musical friends . . . one day be famous." Mildred Spiegel Zucker quoted in Ibid., pp. 74–75.

Page 26: "Do you really think so?" Leonard Bernstein quoted in Ibid., p. 75.

Page 27: "After rehearsals . . . resented." Mildred Spiegel Zucker quoted in Ibid., p. 75.

Page 27: "had a constant conflict." Mildred Spiegel Zucker quoted in Ibid., p. 78.

Page 27: "What's the matter? . . . music like that." Leonard Bernstein to Mildred Spiegel, quoted in Burton, p. 27.

Page 28: "bent over . . . knuckles showing." B. Bernstein, p. 114.

Page 28: "When Sam . . . bloody murder." Leonard Bernstein quoted in Ibid., p. 115.

Page 28: "Having talked . . . every two weeks." Letter from Leonard Bernstein to Helen Coates, October 15, 1932. Leonard Bernstein Collection, Music Division, Library of Congress.

Page 28: "She taught . . . raging fingers." Leonard Bernstein quoted in Burton, p. 25.

Page 32: "quickest learner" Helen Coates quoted in Ibid., p. 25.

Page 32: "gave me . . . piano lessons." L. Bernstein, *Findings*, p. 197.

Page 32: "Will you tell . . . to hear him!" Jennie Bernstein quoted in Burton, p. 27.

Page 34: "I can't seem . . . the coming fall." Leonard Bernstein in a letter to Helen Coates quoted in Ibid., p. 26.

Page 34: "I bought *Bolero*!!! . . . Crash! Discord!" Leonard Bernstein in letters to Sid Ramin, summer 1933, quoted in Ibid., p. 21.

Page 34: "Now even . . . and are silent." Leonard Bernstein in a letter to Helen Coates quoted in Ibid., p. 22.

Page 34: "many of the . . . Boston Symphony Orchestra." Mildred Spiegel Zucker quoted in Mintz, p. 75.

Page 35: "unavoidably detained . . . means of maintenance." Samuel Bernstein in a letter to Helen Coates, 1934, quoted in Burton, p. 27.

Page 36: "using just hit tunes" Leonard Bernstein quoted in Ibid., p. 22.

Page 36: "Guess what? . . . loves hot dogs." Leonard Bernstein's typewritten script, *Carmen*. Leonard Bernstein Collection, Music Division, Library of Congress.

Page 36: "I sang Carmen . . . underwear was showing." Leonard Bernstein quoted in Burton, p. 22.

Page 36: "love of my life" Leonard Bernstein quoted in Ibid., p. 22.

Page 37: "Otherwise . . . gotten it." Leonard Bernstein quoted in Ibid., pp. 22–23.

Page 37: "They had . . . twenty-five cents." Leonard Bernstein quoted in Ibid., p. 23.

Page 37: "We were . . . not a career." Leonard Bernstein quoted in B. Bernstein, p. 128.

Page 37: "excellent means . . . musical life." Essay by Leonard Bernstein, September 24, 1934, pp. 1 and 3. Leonard Bernstein Collection, Music Division, Library of Congress.

Page 39: "It was a . . . double bar [on]." Leonard Bernstein quoted in *Leonard Bernstein: Boston to Broadway: Concerts and Symposia at Harvard University*, p. 39, research credit: Derrick Wang, Harvard '06.

Page 40: "All for one . . . beyond our wall." Leonard Bernstein and Lawrence F. Ebb, Class Song, 1935, Leonard Bernstein Collection, Music Division, Library of Congress.

Page 40: "entire accompaniment" Mildred Speigel Zucker, in Mintz, p. 77.

Page 40: "singing away . . . Lenny's direction from the piano." S. Bernstein, p. 25.

Page 42: "They all laughed . . . all followed him." Jennie Bernstein quoted in Burton, p. 24.

Page 42: "patience was . . . secretly proud." B. Bernstein, p. 128.

Page 42: "It was in . . . liked quiet, relaxing." Jennie Bernstein quoted in Burton, p. 24.

Page 42: "It's *Shabbas* . . . go to *shul!*" Samuel Bernstein quoted in B. Bernstein, p. 129.

Page 43: "Lenny had immediately . . . maid for the day." B. Bernstein, p. 130.

Page 44: "Egyptian dances . . . Twins Kaplan." Program, The Sharon Community Players, August 29, 1936, *Leonard Bernstein: Boston to Broadway: Concerts and Symposia at Harvard University*, 2006, research credit: Shira Brettman, Harvard '07.

Page 44: "During Lenny's . . . spent in Sharon." B. Bernstein, p. 118.

Page 45: "superb musical department there" Leonard Bernstein's essay for Philip Marson at Boston Latin, fall 1934, quoted in Burton, p. 28.

Page 46: "I remember standing . . . And he did." Sid Ramin, "Leonard Bernstein's Boston Years: Team Research in a Harvard Classroom," interviewed February 21, 2006, research credit: Emily Abrams Ansari, Ryan Bañagale, and Corinna Campbell, Harvard graduate students.

Page 46: "concentrate on . . . like economics." B. Bernstein, p. 131.

Page 46: "We knew it . . . and sing it, too." Edwin Geller quoted in Secrest, pp. 39–40.

Page 48: "Hundreds of people . . . tin pans." Monroe Rosenfeld quoted on Parlor Songs Association website, http://parlorsongs.com/insearch/tinpanalley/tinpanalley.php, accessed March 9, 2010.

Page 49: "But when I tried . . . & Sullivan, show tunes." Hal Stubbs, former Sharon resident, in an email to Harvard graduate student Emily Abrams Ansari, March 3, 2006, in connection with *Leonard Bernstein: Boston to Broadway: Concerts and Symposia at Harvard University.*

Page 49: "We played a medley . . . favorite of ours." Sid Ramin, email to author, September 5, 2007.

Page 49: "Lenny had his . . . memory as a crutch." Sid Ramin, "Leonard Bernstein's Boston Years: Team Research in a Harvard Classroom," recorded October 13, 2006, Disc #6, research credit: Emily Abrams Ansari, Ryan Bañagale, and Corinna Campbell, Harvard graduate students.

Page 50: "You could not study . . . in hushed whispers." Leonard Bernstein quoted in Burton, p. 33.

Page 52: "a big cavernous . . . iron beds." Burton Bernstein, "Leonard Bernstein's Boston Years: Team Research in a Harvard Classroom," interviewed February 7, 2006, Audio 1–12, Bernstein Family, track #6, research credit: Emily Abrams Ansari, Ryan Bañagale, and Corinna Campbell, Harvard graduate students.

Page 52: "I could hear . . . second nature to me." Burton Bernstein, Ibid.

Page 52: "great piano teacher . . . magic carpet." L. Bernstein, *Findings*, pp. 196.

Page 52: "I would play . . . I floated out." L. Bernstein, "My Teacher, Heinrich Gebhard," p. 100.

Page 53: "overwhelmed" and "went bananas" Leonard Bernstein quoted in Burton, p. 36.

Page 54: "Mitropoulos was visiting . . . housedress we went." Jennie Bernstein quoted in Peyser, pp. 55–56.

Page 56: "I learned for . . . way he wanted." Leonard Bernstein quoted in Burton, p. 37.

Page 56: "genius boy" Dimitri Mitropoulos quoted in B. Bernstein, p. 134.

Page 56: "You are sensitive . . . fulfill your mission." Dimitri Mitropoulos quoted in Burton, p. 37.

Page 57: "rhythm band" Caption printed on photo, 1937, *The Berkshire Eagle*, Leonard Bernstein Collection, Music Division, Library of Congress.

Page 58: "America's greatest Jewish . . . I was Gershwin." Leonard Bernstein quoted in Burton, p. 38.

Page 60: "clever with words . . . musical memory." Ibid., p. 38.

Page 60: "I Wish . . . in Borneo." Adolph Green quoted in Ibid., p. 39.

Page 60: "I knew as . . . than a genius." Adolph Green quoted in Ibid., p. 39.

Page 62: "Who is that . . . 'crazy artist nuts.'" Samuel Bernstein to Jennie Bernstein quoted in B. Bernstein, p. 126 and p. 125.

Page 62: "He sulked . . . they departed." Ibid., p. 125.

Page 63: "resented Lenny's being serious" Mildred Spiegel Zucker, in Mintz, p. 76.

Page 63: "She asked . . . lectures were held." Ibid., p. 76.

Page 63: "It was raining . . . did crazy things." Ibid., p. 76.

Page 64: "genuine talent" *Boston Herald* quoted in Burton, p. 40.

Page 64: "with an authority . . . unusual talent." *Christian Science Monitor* quoted in Ibid., p. 41.

Page 67: "hollow stupid . . . uninteresting." Leonard Bernstein's class notes, Leonard Bernstein Collection, Music Division, Library of Congress. Used in *Leonard Bernstein: Boston to Broadway: Concerts and Symposia at Harvard University*, 2006, pp. 286 and 287, research credit: Scott Duke Kominers, Harvard '09.

Page 67: "I did my work . . . showed up." Harold Shapero, "Leonard Bernstein's Boston Years: Team Research in a Harvard Classroom," interviewed February 21, 2006, research credit: Emily Abrams Ansari, Ryan Bañagale, and Corinna Campbell, Harvard graduate students.

Page 67: "He played a little . . . 'I like it!'" Harold Shapero, Ibid.

Page 67: "His confidence . . . making mistakes." Harold Shapero, Ibid.

Page 67: "He couldn't . . . often enough." Robert Lubell quoted in Secrest, p. 43.

Page 67: "American sound." Joseph Horowitz, *Classical Music in America*, p. 434.

Page 68: "went crazy . . . dissonant, intoxicating." Leonard Bernstein quoted in Secrest, p. 43.

Page 68: "And he [Prall] . . . for us to go." Leonard Bernstein quoted in Aaron Copland and Vivian Perlis, *Copland: 1900 Through 1942*, p. 336.

Page 68: "teach it back to Lenny" L. Bernstein, "My Teacher, Heinrich Gebhard," p. 100.

Page 68: "trademark . . . and starting it." L. Bernstein, *Findings*, p. 286.

Page 68: "Already in his seat . . . Copland, Leonard Bernstein." Ibid, p. 287.

Page 70: "Aaron Copland's famous . . . he worked." Ibid, p. 287.

Page 70: "It'll ruin your . . . it like that." Leonard Bernstein quoted in Copland and Perlis, p. 337.

Page 70: "I followed the . . . for hours." L. Bernstein, *Findings*, p. 288.

Page 70: "This is good . . . start from there." Aaron Copland quoted in Ibid, p. 288.

Page 70: "Aaron became . . . I ever had." L. Bernstein, Ibid., p. 288.

Page 72: "Stop complaining . . . for success." Aaron Copland quoted in Ibid., p. 290.

Page 74: "Papa, I'm going . . . my life." Leonard Bernstein quoted in Peyser, p. 57.

Page 74: "glimmering possibility" B. Bernstein, p. 134.

Page 74: "Me and My Shadow" Burton, p. 52.

Page 74: "I really feel . . . for conducting." Helen Coates to Leonard Bernstein, July 1939, quoted in Burton, p. 58.

Page 74: "The Absorption . . . American Music." L. Bernstein, *Findings*, p. 37.

Page 74: "The greatest single . . . of the Negroes." Ibid., p. 50.

Page 74: "The earliest . . . rhythms, above all." Ibid., p. 63.

Page 74: "Negro themes," "swing," Ibid., p. 52.

Page 74: "What music of . . . little American stuff." Leonard Bernstein to Aaron Copland, November 19, 1938, quoted in Burton, pp. 50–51.

Page 75: "Composing in . . . you look at it." Aaron Copland to Leonard Bernstein, December 1938, quoted in Ibid., p.51.

Page 75: "in partial . . . of arts." L. Bernstein, *Findings*, p. 37.

Page 76: "The idea of conducting . . . impossible." Leonard Bernstein, transcript of source interviews for *Reflections*, Sound Roll #1, p.1.

Page 76: "No money . . . no ideas." Leonard Bernstein to Ken Ehrman quoted in Burton, p. 51.

Page 77: "barely enough . . . last fling." B. Bernstein, p. 134.

Page 78: "glorious Steinway grand . . . my heart's content." Leonard Bernstein to Helen Coates, July 1939, quoted in Burton, p. 57.

Page 78: "around 3 A.M . . . back to sleep." Betty Comden quoted in Ibid., p. 58.

Page 78: "I went home . . . my legs." Leonard Bernstein quoted in Peyser, p. 63.

Page 79: "prime victims" B. Bernstein, p. 88.

Page 79: "Sometimes Sam . . . afternoon dinner." B. Bernstein, Ibid., p. 87.

Page 80: "I've finished Harvard . . . What shall I do?" Leonard Bernstein quoted in Peyser, pp. 64–65.

Page 80: "I know what . . . a conductor." Leonard Bernstein quoting Dimitri Mitropoulos in Ibid., p. 65.

Page 80: "gifts . . . Me? A conductor? . . . the Juilliard School." Leonard Bernstein, transcript of source interviews for *Reflections*, Roll #1, A–8.

Page 81: "Can something be . . . possibility of Curtis?" Leonard Bernstein to Aaron Copland, July 30, 1939, quoted in Burton, p. 59.

Page 81: "Any day on . . . too sick to conduct." Quote in Horowitz, p. 308.

Page 81: "I had never really . . . of conducting them." Leonard Bernstein, transcript of source interviews for *Reflections*, Roll #1, A–9.

Page 82: "I could barely see . . . see the title." Leonard Bernstein, Ibid., Roll #1, A–9.

Page 82: "Do you know . . . this piece." L. Bernstein, *Findings*, pp. 204–205.

Page 84: "Not one more cent for music." Samuel Bernstein quoted in S. Bernstein, p. 42.

Page 85: "city of . . . and horror." Leonard Bernstein quoted in Burton, p. 64.

Page 85: "ultimate powers . . . expense money." B. Bernstein, p. 135.

Page 85: "My father gave . . . for Curtis students." Leonard Bernstein quoted in Copland and Perlis, p. 340.

Page 87: "I feel happy . . . of Mr. Reiner." Dimitri Mitropoulos quoted in Burton, p. 65.

Page 87: "It looks like . . . I am studying." Leonard Bernstein to Helen Coates, October 17, 1939, quoted in Ibid., p. 64.

Page 87: "Fritz . . . Yes, Mr. Bernstein.'" Ibid., p. 66.

Page 87: "still in short pants" L. Bernstein, *Findings*, p. 323.

Page 87: "I seem to be . . . *mould* them." Leonard Bernstein to Helen Coates, October 17, 1939, quoted in Burton, p. 65.

Page 88: "the greatest piano . . . than Serkin." Ibid., p. 65.

Page 88: "She is a veritable . . . will please her." Ibid., p. 66.

Page 88: "Why are you banging . . . absolutely trembling." Ibid., pp. 66–67.

Page 88: "It seems she is . . . pianist of me." Leonard Bernstein to Helen Coates, November 7, 1939, quoted in Ibid, p. 66.

Page 88: "She would have . . . class unprepared." Lukas Foss quoted in Ibid, p. 65.

Page 88: "It's a dream . . . except sleep plenty." Leonard Bernstein to Helen Coates, October 17, 1939, quoted in Ibid, p. 65.

Page 90: "They regarded me . . . as sight reading." L. Bernstein, *Findings*, pp. 323–324.

Page 90: "I just adore . . . Except music!" Leonard Bernstein in Gruen, p. 51.

Page 90: "I remember taking . . . his heart out." Phyllis Moss quoted in Burton, p. 68

Page 90: "he never struck . . . miserable to me." Lukas Foss quoted in Ibid., pp. 68–69.

Page 92: "Lenny was at . . . had inherited it." Shirley Gabis Perle quoted in Ibid., p. 85.

Page 92: "Lenny would tear . . . We did." Shirley Gabis Perle quoted in Peyser, p. 71.

Page 94: "make a hundred . . . beauty supply business." Shirley Gabis Perle quoted in Ibid., p. 72.

Page 96: "There I was . . . a wonderful shock." Leonard Bernstein quoted in Peyser, p. 77.

Page 96: "Such an explosion in my life" Leonard Bernstein quoted in Copland and Perlis, p. 340.

Page 96: "Their room . . . at Tanglewood." An unnamed contemporary quoted in Peyser, p. 82.

Page 96: "I did this . . . couldn't repeat it." Leonard Bernstein quoted in Burton, p. 76.

Page 99: "He became like . . . born in Russia." Leonard Bernstein quoted in Peyser, p. 80.

Page 99: "Look, it's like a pencil." Leonard Bernstein quoted in Burton, p. 77.

Page 99: "Dearest Folks— . . . All my love, Lenny." Leonard Bernstein to his parents, July 11, 1940, quoted in B. Bernstein, pp. 136–137.

Page 100: "When Sam finally . . . for him alone." Ibid., p. 138.

Page 102: "Learn from . . . complete your obligation." Telegram from Serge Koussevitzky to Leonard Bernstein, October 1, 1940, quoted in Burton, p. 81.

Page 103: "On the other . . . wars at all." Leonard Bernstein quoted in Peyser, p. 90.

Page 103: "Thanks be . . . go to war." Samuel Bernstein quoted in Ibid., p. 90.

Page 104: "under neutral colors" B. Bernstein, p. 88.

Page 104: "rich brats" Leonard Bernstein quoted in Burton, p. 87.

Page 104: "clean copy" Ibid., p. 84.

Page 104: "Your idea . . . over several points." Aaron Copland to Leonard Bernstein, November 1940, quoted in Ibid., p. 84.

Page 106: "La Tirana" Leonard Bernstein quoted in Ibid., p. 87.

Page 106: "was a very great teacher" Leonard Bernstein, transcript of source interviews for *Reflections*, B-14.

Page 106: "He demanded . . . had to do." Leonard Bernstein quoted in Peyser, p. 84.

Page 106: "It was hard . . . inspirational." Leonard Bernstein, transcript of source interviews for *Reflections*, Roll #2, B-12.

Page 106: "*Bravo!—a thousand times!*" Helen Coates to Leonard Bernstein, April 26, 1941, quoted in Burton, p. 90.

Page 107: "Lukas Foss would . . . like Lukas Foss." Leonard Bernstein quoted in transcript of source interviews for *Reflections*, Roll #2, B-13.

Page 108: "it (the overture) brought down . . . than Kouss had gotten . . . 'Bravo.'" Leonard Bernstein to Mildred Spiegel, July 1941, quoted in Burton, p. 93.

Page 108: "The black pins . . . east toward Moscow." B. Bernstein, p. 97.

Page 108: "If the stories . . . evil was impossible." Ibid., p. 97.

Page 111: "My family . . . on the front seat" Ibid., p. 97.

Page 111: "They tried, in—French—anything." Ibid., p. 94.

Page 111: "Try, Dinah, try to be kind . . . " Leonard Bernstein, lyric sheet in pencil. Leonard Bernstein Collection, Music Division, Library of Congress.

Page 112: "I cannot be given . . . field of endeavor." Leonard Bernstein to Serge Koussevitzky, August 1941, quoted in Burton, p. 95.

Page 112: "Modern music is . . . but I don't." Leonard Bernstein, transcript of source interviews for *Reflections*, Roll #2, B–14.

Page 112: "How would you . . . the Boston Symphony?" Ibid., B–15.

Page 112: "I had to have . . . the Boston Symphony." Ibid., B–15.

Page 113: "a well-tutored . . . the family business." Burton Bernstein, author's interview, April 18, 2007.

Page 113: "But he wanted . . . it for him." Samuel Bernstein quoted in Peyser, p. 94.

Page 113: "wangled enough money . . . on Huntington Avenue." B. Bernstein, p. 138.

Page 113: "I thought that . . . support myself." Leonard Bernstein, transcript of source interviews for *Reflections*, Roll #2, B-15.

Page 114: "making Lenny a . . . Sam was right." B. Bernstein, pp. 138–139.

Page 114: "Nobody was interested . . . at that point." Leonard Bernstein, transcript of source interviews for *Reflections*, Roll #2, B-16.

Page 114: "He was a . . . place to go." B. Bernstein, p. 138.

Page 115: "It was magnificent." Leonard Bernstein, transcript of source interviews for *Reflections*, Roll #2, B-16.

Page 115: "turned out in thousands" Burton, p. 99.

Page 115: "At the end . . . in New York." Leonard Bernstein, transcript of source interviews for *Reflections*, Roll #2, B-17.

Page 116: "the Big City . . . for a job." Ibid., B-18.

Page 116: "Now I know . . . so very bright." Lenny Amber arrangement, sheet music, Leonard Bernstein Collection, Music Division, Library of Congress.

Page 116: "Bernstein . . . means 'amberstone.'" S. Bernstein, p. 59.

Page 116: "That job . . . time to compose." B. Bernstein, p. 140.

Page 117: "from lack of sleep . . . only half done." S. Bernstein, p. 60.

Page 117: "But it won . . . dedication to him." B. Bernstein, p. 140.

Page 118: "I would walk . . . la de da de da." Edys Merrill quoted in Peyser, p. 101.

Page 118: "I hate music! . . . la dee la dee da dee." Leonard Bernstein, score, *Kid Songs* (I Hate Music), No. III, Leonard Bernstein Collection, Music Division, Library of Congress.

Page 119: "great success" Leonard Bernstein to Helen Coates, February 19, 1943, quoted in Burton, p. 104.

Page 119: "It's all . . . where's the money?" Lukas Foss quoted in Ibid., p. 105.

Page 119: "boring jobs" Leonard Bernstein, transcript of source interviews for *Reflections*, Roll #2, B-19.

Page 119: "He had no . . . on his own." Edys Merrill quoted in Peyser, p. 100.

Page 119: "Lovely, lovely . . . too sad." Leonard Bernstein to Aaron Copland, June 1943, quoted in Burton, p. 107.

Page 120: "same criticism . . . something else." Ibid., p. 107.

Page 120: "Please let me . . . your military status." Artur Rodzinski to Leonard Bernstein, March 10, 1943, quoted in Ibid., p. 106.

Page 120: "I am very . . . talk about it." Artur Rodzinski to Leonard Bernstein, April 7, 1943, quoted in Ibid., p. 106.

Page 120: "He was also . . . feeling quite Jewish." Leonard Bernstein, transcript of source interviews for *Reflections*, 45-A, Sound Five.

Page 120: "as bleak . . . in the musical world." Ibid, Roll #2, B-21.

Page 122: "I have been through . . . 'Take Bernstein.'" Ibid., Roll #3, A-3, p. 24.

Page 122: "I freaked out . . . have a real job." Leonard Bernstein quoted in Peyser, pp. 106–107.

Page 125: "not to hold their breath" B. Bernstein, p. 141.

Page 127: "no conductor . . . gotten sick." Leonard Bernstein, transcript of source interviews for *Reflections*, 45-A, Sound Five, A-8, p. 29.

Page 127: "no one ever . . . considered very young." Ibid., A-6, p. 27.

Page 127: "wildly excited . . . demanded the family's . . . unusually atremble." B. Bernstein, p. 142.

Page 127: "snowbound Stockbridge" Burton, p. 114.

Page 127: "I was thrilled." Leonard Bernstein, transcript of source interviews for *Reflections*, 45-A, Sound Five, A-9, p. 30.

Page 128: "uncomfortable . . . 'artist people.'" B. Bernstein, p. 143.

Page 128: "You have to . . . this afternoon." Leonard Bernstein quoted in Burton, p. 115.

Page 128: "I was scared out of my wits." Leonard Bernstein quoted in Secrest, p. 117.

Page 128: "There was no time for me to rehearse." Leonard Bernstein, transcript of source interviews for *Reflections*, 45-A, Sound Five, A-11, p. 32.

Page 128: "He, Lenny Bernstein . . . that very afternoon." B. Bernstein, p. 144.

Page 128: "*Oy, gevalt!*" Samuel and Jennie Bernstein quoted in Ibid., p. 144.

Page 128: "Wish me luck . . . at intermission." Leonard Bernstein quoted in Ibid., p. 144.

Page 129: "majesty and immensity . . . knew it then or not." B. Bernstein, Ibid., p. 145.

Page 129: "to witness the . . . in this country." Bruno Zirato quoted in Ibid., p. 145.

Page 129: "He meant my brother." B. Bernstein, Ibid., p. 145.

Page 129: "'cutaway' . . . only presentable . . . sharkskin." Burton, p. 116.

Page 129: "He sort of hopped . . . what he was doing." B. Bernstein, pp. 145–146.

Page 129: "I remember giving . . . all a dream." Leonard Bernstein, transcript of source interviews for *Reflections*, Side B, Sound Roll #4, B-13, p. 34.

Page 130: "With those first . . . almost immediately." S. Bernstein, p. 72.

Page 130: "A lot of important-looking . . . But I was proud." B. Bernstein, p. 146.

Page 130: "from Lenny banging . . . piano at home." Ibid., p. 146.

Page 130: "The orchestra was . . . all their attention." Leonard Bernstein quoted in Secrest, p. 118.

Page 130: "There was a . . . roar of applause." S. Bernstein, p. 73.

Page 130: "The house roared . . . front of the stage." B. Bernstein, p. 146.

Page 131: "stood up and . . . that kind of music." Jacques Margolies quoted in Secrest, p. 118.

Page 131: "Once he waved . . . everybody stared." B. Bernstein, p. 147.

Page 131: "absolutely dazzled . . . very deep emotion." Leonard Bernstein, transcript of source interviews for *Reflections*, Side B, Roll #4, B-15, p. 36.

Page 133: "I'm very proud of him." Jennie Bernstein quoted in B. Bernstein, p. 147.

Page 133: "Just the other day . . . for that." Samuel Bernstein quoted in Ibid., p. 147.

Page 133: "I couldn't believe . . . I was famous." Leonard Bernstein, transcript of source interviews for *Reflections*, B-15, p. 36.

Page 133: "Young aide leads Philharmonic." *New York Times* headline quoted in Burton, p. 117.

Page 133: "brilliant" and "exciting." S. Bernstein, p. 74.

Page 133: "It's a good American . . . Gets His Chance." Burton, p. 117.

Page 133: "How could I . . . be Leonard Bernstein?" Samuel Bernstein quoted in Ibid., p. 122.

Page 135: "that it would . . . tumbling down." B. Bernstein, p. 151.

Page 136: "hear with new ears" Leonard Bernstein in Young People's Concert, December 13, 1958.

Page 136: "Lenny made it possible." Burton Bernstein, author's interview, April 18, 2007.

Page 140: "full of enthusiasm and fun" Betty Comden quoted in Burton, p. 58.

Page 141: "to keep up . . . of working." Betty Comden quoted in obituary by Robert Berkvist, *New York Times*, November 24, 2006, p. A21.

Page 142: "authentic genius" Leonard Bernstein, transcript of source interviews for *Reflections*, Side B, Sound Roll #2, B-13, p. 13.

Page 142: "He slept under . . . in the apartment." Cornelia Brendel Foss quoted in "Encores: Revisiting 'The Prairie'" by Rebecca Mead, *The New Yorker*, July 23, 2007, p. 24.

Page 143: "'I'm still upright . . . upright and grand.'" Burton, p. 521.

Page 143: "a crazy artist nut" Samuel Bernstein quoted in B. Bernstein, p. 125.

Page 146: "orchestration . . . in consultations" Sid Ramin, author's interview, August 22, 2007.

Page 147: "In the midst . . . on the floor." Sid Ramin, "Leonard Bernstein's Boston Years: Team Research in a Harvard Classroom," February 21, 2006, research credit: Emily Abrams Ansari, Ryan Bañagale, and Corinna Campbell, Harvard graduate students.

Page 147: "I don't think . . . the way it was." Sid Ramin, Ibid.

Page 147: "impossibly high standards" L. Bernstein, *Findings*, pp. 202.

Page 148: "You were cheated! . . . your money back!" Fritz Reiner quoted in Horowitz, p. 308.

Page 148: "supreme master . . . the composer wanted." L. Bernstein, *Findings*, pp. 202–203.

Page 148: "very good friends." Leonard Bernstein, transcript of source interviews for *Reflections*, Side B, Sound Roll #2, B-12, p. 12.

Page 149: "You don't expect . . . be another composer." Harold Shapero, "Leonard Bernstein's Boston Years: Team Research in a Harvard Classroom," October 13, 2006, Disc #6, research credit: Emily Abrams Ansari, Ryan Bañagale, and Corinna Campbell, Harvard graduate students.

Page 150: "We quickly became . . . tuner had to replace." Mildred Spiegel Zucker, in Mintz, pp. 74–75.

Page 150: "Lenny sent eighty-four . . . be another Lenny." Ibid., p. 80.

Page 150: "With all my heart . . . June 12, 1937." Ibid., p. 76.

Page 150: "He also wrote . . . played at Harvard." Ibid., p. 76.

Page 152: "a series of notes . . . effect on us." L. Bernstein, *Findings*, p. 107.

Page 152: "We 'abstract' artists . . . Have fun." Ibid., p. 107.

Photo Credits and Permissions

Photo Credits

Cover: Library of Congress, Music Division, Leonard Bernstein Collection.

p. i: Library of Congress, Music Division, Leonard Bernstein Collection.

pp. ii–iii: Library of Congress, Music Division, Leonard Bernstein Collection.

p. vi: Library of Congress, Music Division, Leonard Bernstein Collection.

p. viii: Library of Congress, Music Division, Leonard Bernstein Collection.

p. xi: Library of Congress, Music Division, Leonard Bernstein Collection.

p. xii: Library of Congress, Music Division, Leonard Bernstein Collection.

p. xiv: Library of Congress, Music Division, Leonard Bernstein Collection.

p. 2: Library of Congress, Music Division, Leonard Bernstein Collection.

p. 4: Library of Congress, Music Division, Leonard Bernstein Collection.

p. 5: From the archives of Congregation Mishkan Tefila. Used in *Leonard Bernstein: Boston to Broadway: Concerts and Symposia at Harvard University,* research credit: Lily Yeh, Harvard graduate student. Image courtesy of the Edna Kuhn Loeb Music Library, Harvard University.

p. 6: Library of Congress, Music Division, Leonard Bernstein Collection.

p. 7: Library of Congress, Music Division, Leonard Bernstein Collection.

p. 12: From the archives at New England Conservatory, Boston, MA. Used in *Leonard Bernstein: Boston to Broadway: Concerts and Symposia at Harvard University,* research credit: Stephanie Lai, Harvard '06.

p. 15: Library of Congress, Music Division, Leonard Bernstein Collection.

p. 17: Library of Congress, Music Division, Leonard Bernstein Collection.

p. 18: Library of Congress, Music Division, Leonard Bernstein Collection.

p. 19: From the archives of Congregation Mishkan Tefila. Used in *Leonard Bernstein: Boston to Broadway: Concerts and Symposia at Harvard University,* research credit: Stephanie Samuels, Harvard '06. Image courtesy of the Edna Kuhn Loeb Music Library, Harvard University.

p. 23: Library of Congress, Music Division, Leonard Bernstein Collection.

p. 26: Library of Congress, Music Division, Leonard Bernstein Collection.

p. 29: Library of Congress, Music Division, Leonard Bernstein Collection.

pp. 30–31: Library of Congress, Music Division, Leonard Bernstein Collection.

p. 35: Library of Congress, Music Division, Leonard Bernstein Collection.

p. 37: Library of Congress, Music Division, Leonard Bernstein Collection.

p. 38: Library of Congress, Music Division, Leonard Bernstein Collection.

pp. 40–41: Class Song by Leonard Bernstein and Lawrence F. Ebb. Reprinted by permission of the Leonard Bernstein Music Publishing Company LLC, publisher, and Boosey & Hawkes, Inc., sole agent. Used in *Leonard Bernstein: Boston to Broadway: Concerts and Symposia at Harvard University,* research credit: Derrick Wang, Harvard '06.

p. 42: Courtesy of Robert and Ruth Potash. Used in *Leonard Bernstein: Boston to Broadway: Concerts and Symposia at Harvard University,* research credit: Shira Brettman, Harvard '07.

p. 44: Courtesy of Robert and Ruth Potash. Used in *Leonard Bernstein: Boston to Broadway: Concerts and Symposia at Harvard University,* research credit: Shira Brettman, Harvard '07.

p. 47: Library of Congress, Music Division, Leonard Bernstein Collection.

p. 48: Library of Congress, Farm Security Administration and Office of War Information Collection.

p. 50: Library of Congress, Music Division, Leonard Bernstein Collection. Used in *Leonard Bernstein: Boston to Broadway: Concerts and Symposia at Harvard University,* research credit: Emily Abrams Ansari and Ryan Bañagale, Harvard graduate students.

p. 51: Library of Congress, Music Division, Leonard Bernstein Collection. Used in *Leonard Bernstein: Boston to Broadway: Concerts and Symposia at Harvard University,* research credit: Emily Abrams Ansari and Ryan Bañagale, Harvard graduate students.

p. 55: Library of Congress, Music Division, Leonard Bernstein Collection.

p. 58: Library of Congress, Music Division, Leonard Bernstein Collection. Courtesy of the *Berkshire Eagle.*

p. 59: Library of Congress, Prints and Photographs Division, Carl Van Vechten Collection.

p. 61: Library of Congress, Music Division, Leonard Bernstein Collection.

p. 65: Library of Congress, Music Division, Leonard Bernstein Collection. Used in *Leonard Bernstein: Boston to Broadway: Concerts and Symposia at Harvard University,* research credit: Scott Duke Kominers, Harvard '09.

p. 66: Library of Congress, Music Division, Leonard Bernstein Collection. Used in *Leonard Bernstein: Boston to Broadway: Concerts and Symposia at Harvard University,* research credit: Scott Duke Kominers, Harvard '09.

p. 69: Library of Congress, Music Division, Leonard Bernstein Collection.

p. 71: String Trio sketch by Leonard Bernstein. Reprinted by permission of the Leonard Bernstein Music Publishing Company LLC, publisher, and Boosey & Hawkes, Inc., sole agent.

p. 75: Library of Congress, Music Division, Leonard Bernstein Collection.

p. 79: Library of Congress, Music Division, Leonard Bernstein Collection.

p. 83: Library of Congress, Music Division, Leonard Bernstein Collection.

p. 86: Courtesy of the Curtis Institute of Music.

p. 89: Courtesy of the Curtis Institute of Music.

p. 91: Courtesy of the Curtis Institute of Music.

p. 92: Courtesy of Shirley Gabis Perle. Photographer: Adrian Siegel.

p. 93: Courtesy of Shirley Gabis Perle.

p. 95: Library of Congress, Music Division, Leonard Bernstein Collection.

p. 97: Library of Congress, Music Division, Leonard Bernstein Collection.

p. 98: Library of Congress, Music Division, Leonard Bernstein Collection. Courtesy of the *Berkshire Eagle.*

p. 101: Library of Congress, Music Division, Leonard Bernstein Collection.

p. 105: Library of Congress, Music Division, Leonard Bernstein Collection.

p. 107: Library of Congress, Music Division, Leonard Bernstein Collection.

p. 109: Library of Congress, Music Division, Leonard Bernstein Collection.

p. 110: Library of Congress, Music Division, Leonard Bernstein Collection.

p. 113: Library of Congress, Music Division, Leonard Bernstein Collection.

p. 118: *I Hate Music* by Leonard Bernstein. © Copyright 1943 by Mitmark & Sons. Renewed Warner Bros., Inc. Leonard Bernstein Music Publishing Company LLC, publisher. Boosey & Hawkes, Inc., sole agent. All rights reserved. Reprinted by permission.

p. 121: Library of Congress, Music Division, Leonard Bernstein Collection.

p. 123: Library of Congress, Music Division, Leonard Bernstein Collection.

p. 126: Library of Congress, Music Division, Leonard Bernstein Collection.

p. 131: Library of Congress, Music Division, Leonard Bernstein Collection.

p. 132: *The New York Times*/Redux.

p. 134: Library of Congress, Music Division, Leonard Bernstein Collection.

p. 137: Library of Congress, Music Division, Leonard Bernstein Collection.

p. 140, top: Library of Congress, Music Division, Leonard Bernstein Collection.

p. 140, bottom: Library of Congress, Music Division, Leonard Bernstein Collection.

p. 141: Library of Congress, Music Division, Leonard Bernstein Collection.

p. 142: Library of Congress, Music Division, Leonard Bernstein Collection.

p. 143: Library of Congress, Music Division, Leonard Bernstein Collection.

p. 144: Library of Congress, Music Division, Leonard Bernstein Collection.

p. 145: Library of Congress, Music Division, Leonard Bernstein Collection.

p. 146: Library of Congress, Music Division, Leonard Bernstein Collection.

p. 147: Library of Congress, Music Division, Leonard Bernstein Collection.

p. 148: Courtesy of the Robert D. Farber University Archives & Special Collections Department, Brandeis University.

p. 150: Library of Congress, Music Division, Leonard Bernstein Collection.

Text Credits

pp. 10, 11, 14, 19, 76, 80, 81, 82, 106, 107, 112, 113, 114, 115, 116, 119, 120, 122, 127, 128, 129, 131, 133, 142, 148: Letters by Leonard Bernstein © Amberson Holdings LLC. Used by permission of the Leonard Bernstein Office, Inc.

pp. 22, 32, 52, 68, 70, 72, 74, 75, 82, 87, 90, 147, 148, 152: Quotations from Leonard Bernstein's published works (see bibliography) used by permission of Joy Harris Literary Agency, Inc.

pp. 3, 6, 11, 13, 16, 17, 21, 28, 39, 42, 43, 44, 46, 56, 62, 74, 77, 79, 85, 99, 100, 104, 108, 111, 113, 114, 116, 117, 125, 127, 128, 129, 130, 131, 133, 135, 143: Quotations from *Family Matters* by Burton Bernstein. Used with permission.

pp. 25, 40, 84, 116, 117, 130, 133: Quotations from *Making Music* by Shirley Bernstein. By courtesy of Encyclopaedia Britannica, Inc., copyright © 1963. Used with permission.

pp. 1, 3, 4, 9, 10, 11, 14, 20, 24, 25, 27, 28, 32, 34, 35, 36, 37, 42, 45, 50, 53, 56, 58, 60, 64, 74, 75, 76, 78, 81, 85, 87, 88, 90, 92, 96, 99, 102, 104, 106, 108, 112, 115, 119, 120, 127, 128, 129, 133, 140, 143: Quotations from *Leonard Bernstein* by Humphrey Burton. Used with permission.

pp. 20, 22, 25, 46, 68, 128, 130, 131: Quotations from *Leonard Bernstein: A Life* by Meryle Secrest. Used with permission.

pp. 25, 26, 27, 34, 40, 52, 63, 150: Quotations from *My Friend Lenny: A Memoir of My Life in Music* by Ouida Blatt Mintz. Used with permission.

pp. 5, 14, 18, 39, 44, 46, 49, 52, 67, 147, 149: Quotations from *Leonard Bernstein: Boston to Broadway: Concerts and Symposia at Harvard University, 2006.* See source notes for individual student research credits.

Acknowledgments

Many people helped me bring this book to life. First I want to express my sincerest thanks to Jamie Bernstein, Alexander Bernstein, and Nina Bernstein Simmons for their warm interest and cooperation. I am grateful to Burton Bernstein for talking to me over the phone and adding insights into his brother's career. At the Leonard Bernstein Office I am deeply indebted to Craig Urquhart, vice president, public relations and promotion, and to Marie Carter, vice president, licensing & publishing. I also want to thank Sid Ramin for generously sharing anecdotes and explanations of musical terms through emails and phone conversations.

My thanks to the Bernstein family and the Leonard Bernstein Office for putting me in touch with Carol J. Oja, William Powell Mason Professor of Music, and Kay Kaufman Shelemay, G. Gordon Watts Professor of Music, at Harvard University. This book draws extensively from interviews and research conducted by their students in a Harvard seminar they team-taught entitled, "Before *West Side Story*: Leonard Bernstein's Boston." I am enormously grateful to them for allowing me to visit the Eda Kuhn Loeb Music Library at Harvard to view the exhibit and to access an in-house website containing materials gathered by their amazing and dedicated students. I am also grateful to them for permitting me to draw a number of documents from the program book for *Leonard Bernstein: Boston to Broadway: Concerts and Symposia at Harvard University, 2006.* At the Harvard Music Library I wish to thank Sarah Adams, Keeper of the Isham Memorial Library, and Liza Vick, Music Reference and Research Services Librarian. I also want to thank Professor Jonathan D. Sarna at Brandeis University for his helpful information about Bernstein and the Boston Jewish Community of his youth.

My deepest thanks to my friend, Lynn Rosenberg, for her hospitality during the week I was researching at Harvard. And a huge thank you to Walter M. Newman for sharing historical facts and vintage photographs of Sharon, Massachusetts. I also want to thank Robert Potash and Ruth Potash Samit for coming to my aid at the last minute and correcting details about musical summers in Sharon.

One of the high points of this project was spending a day at the Music Division, Library of Congress in Washington, D.C. I thank Mark Horowitz, senior music specialist, for helping me examine music manuscripts and photographs in the Bernstein Collection.

This book would never have happened without the enthusiasm of Yolanda Scott, editorial director of Charlesbridge, who loved the idea right from the start. My best thanks to my editor, Emily Mitchell, for her knowledge of music as well as young people's literature, and for her cheerful guidance throughout this project. And I am grateful to Diane Earley for her stunning book design.

My list of acknowledgments would be incomplete without mentioning my agent, friend, and mentor, George Nicholson, for whom a life without music would be truly unthinkable.

As always I am indebted to my dear friends and colleagues, "Lunch Bunch," for their helpful critiques and enjoyment of young Leonard Bernstein. I appreciate the interest of Merryl Goldberg, professor of music at

California State University, San Marcos, and director of Center ARTES (Art, Research, Teaching, Education, and Schools) who encouraged me to write a book about Leonard Bernstein for young people, and loaned me some of her own precious volumes as I began research.

Lastly, I thank my husband, Michael Rubin, from the bottom of my heart for his unfailing support and encouragement.

Index

Page numbers in *italics* refer to illustrations.

Age of Anxiety (Bernstein), 135
Aida (Verdi), 24, 44
American Federation of Musicians, 112
American Festival Overture (Schuman), 107–108
Appalachian Spring (Copland), 142
Aristophanes, 74
Auden, W. H., 135

Bach, Johann Sebastian, 11, 22, 52, 78, 88
Barber, Samuel, 145
Barbirolli, John, 84
Bartók, Béla, 147
Battleship Potemkin, 64
Beethoven, Ludwig van, 21, 52, 78, 81, 150, 151
Berkshire Music Center, *see* Tanglewood
Bernstein, Alexander (son), 136
Bernstein, Burton "Burtie" (brother), 16, 17, *17,* 42, 43, 44, 52, 62, 77, 80, 85, 100, 108, 111, 113, 114, 116, 117, 125, 127–133, 135, 136
Bernstein, Clara (aunt), 9, 19, 24, 33, 104
Bernstein, Dinah (grandmother), 79, 103–104, 111
Bernstein, Jamie (daughter), ix–xi, *xi,* 136
Bernstein, Jennie (mother), 1, *2,* 6–8, *7,* 16–17, 24, 25, 34, 35, 42, 43, 52, 54, 62, 100, 108, 111, 127–133
   supportiveness of Leonard, 13, 17, 32, 34
Bernstein, Leonard, *i, ii–iii, vi, viii, xi, xii, xiv, 2, 4, 7, 18, 19, 23, 35, 38, 47, 58, 75, 79, 91, 93, 97, 98, 101, 105, 107, 109, 110, 121, 123, 132, 134,*

137; see also Boston Latin School; Harvard University
   allergies and asthma of, 3, 82, 103, 111–112
   as composer, 39, 67, 70–72, 73, 76, 116–118, 119–120, 135, 150
   as conductor, 54, 56, 58, 73–75, 76, 80–84, 85–87, 96–100, 106–108, 119, 120–124, 125–133, 135–136, 142, 145–146, 149, 150, 151
   death of, 136, 141, 142, 143
   discography of, 152–154
   elementary school and, 9–10
   first public performance by, 22
   Judaism and, x, 3–5, 19, 45, 49, 64, 117, 127
   as Lenny Amber, 116
   as pianist, 9, 10–14, 22–26, 27–32, 33–35, 37, 39, 46, 49, 52, 54, 58–59, 63, 64, 67, 68, 70, 76, 78, 87–88, 92, 104, 106–107, 112, 116, 119, 127, 128, 135, 144, 149, 150
   as piano teacher, 14–15, 24, 49, 52–53, 104, 113–114, 116, 135, 146
   timeline of life of, 138–139
Bernstein, Nina (daughter), 136
Bernstein, Samuel (father), 1, *2,* 5–6, *7, 8,* 16–20, *17, 18,* 21–22, *38,* 45, 46, 62, 77, 79–80, 100, 103–104, 108, 111, 117, 120, 125, 127–128, 130–133, 135, 143
   concerns about Leonard's music career, x, 10, 11–13, 17–18, 21, 25, 27, 28, 34–36, 37–39, 42, 46, 52, 63, 74, 84, 85, 94, 99, 112–114, 119, 135

religiousness of, 3, 5, 13, 33, 42, 64, 117
Bernstein, Shirley Anne (sister),
    3, 4, 7, 10, 16, 24–25, 36, 39, 43–44, 44, 52, 84,
    94, 100, 111, 116, 117, 122, 127, 128, 130, 140
Bernstein, Shlomo (uncle), 104
Bernstein, Yudel (grandfather), 79, 103–104, 111
Billy the Kid (Copland), 92, 142
Birds, The, 74
Bizet, Georges, 24
Bolero (Ravel), 20, 21, 34, 42
Boston Latin School, 16, 19, 25, 36, 37, 39, 45
    1935 class song of, 39, 40–41
Boston Pops, 20
Boston Public School Orchestra, 34, 150
Boston Symphony Orchestra, 27, 34, 53, 84, 94,
    107, 112, 115, 144–145, 149, 150
Brahms, Johannes, 52, 78, 82, 106
Braslavsky, Solomon, 4–5, 5
Briggs and Briggs, 67, 149
Brooklyn, New York, 67, 104, 141

Caesar, Irving, 116
Camp Onota, 57–60, 58, 143
Candide (Bernstein), 135, 151
Carmen (Bizet), 24, 36–37
Carnegie Hall, ix, xi, 116, 124, 125–129, 134, 136,
    137, 140
Chávez, Carlos, 112
Chicago Symphony Orchestra, 148
Chopin, Frédéric, 11, 22, 54
Cincinnati Symphony, 81, 147–148
Cleveland Orchestra, 122
Coates, Helen, 23, 28–32, 29, 34–35, 74, 78, 87,
    88, 98, 106, 119, 140, 140
Comden, Betty, 78, 79, 140–141, 140, 143–144
Congregation Adath Sharon, 33
Copland, Aaron, 67–72, 69, 73, 74–75, 81, 92, 94–
    96, 104, 105, 107–108, 116, 117, 119, 141–142,
    141, 144–145, 149, 150, 151
Curtis Institute of Music, 81–92, 96, 99, 100–102,
    104–106, 107, 119, 122, 142, 147, 148

Debussy, Claude, 52, 60
Delancey Pharmacy, 92
Die Meistersinger (Wagner), 130
Don Quixote (Strauss), 130, 133

Ebb, Lawrence F., 39, 40
El Salon Mexico (Copland), 67–68, 104, 151
Extension of a Theme by Adolph Green (Bernstein),
    119

Fancy Free (Bernstein), 135, 144, 151
Fiedler, Arthur, 20, 27
Fingal's Cave (Mendelssohn), 53
Foss, Christopher, 143
Foss, Cornelia Brendel, 142
Foss, Lukas, 88, 90, 96, 97, 107, 119, 142–143, 142
Frederics Permanent Wave machine, 6, 6

Gabis, Shirley, 90–92, 92, 94
Gebhard, Heinrich, 28, 52, 53, 63, 68, 74
Geller, Edwin, 46
Gershwin, George, 14, 22, 49, 52, 57, 58–59, 59,
    74, 145
Gilbert and Sullivan, 39, 43, 46, 49, 60
"Good Night, Sweetheart," 10, 14
Gordon, Beatrice, 36, 37
Gould, Morton, 27
Great Depression, ix, 22
Green, Adolph, 60–62, 61, 77–78, 79, 116, 119,
    140–141, 143–144, 143
Grieg, Edvard, 24, 33, 34

Harvard University, 45–46, 48, 49–50, 53, 63,
    64–67, 68, 70, 74–76, 77, 80, 90, 96, 145, 146,
    148–149
    Eliot House at, 64, 70
    Greek Society at, 54, 74
    Leonard's coursework at, 50, 51, 64–67, 65, 66,
    74–75
Hasty Pudding Theatricals, 49
Hawkins, Coleman, 116
Hitler, Adolf, 77, 108, 120

H.M.S. Pinafore (Gilbert and Sullivan), 43, 44
Holliday, Judy, 143

I Hate Music (Bernstein), 117–118, *118*, 122, 127
"I Wish That I'd Been Born in Borneo," 60

jazz, 46, 74, 116
Jeremiah (Bernstein), 117, 119–120, 135
Jiampietro, Lelia, 43–44, *44*
Juilliard School, 80–81

Karp, Frieda, 10–11
Kern, Jerome, 49
Kid Songs, see I Hate Music (Bernstein)
klezmer music, 13, 18, 28
Kostal, Irwin, 146
Koussevitzky, Serge, 27, 84,
     94–102, *95*, *97*, *98*, 106, 108, *109*, 111–112, 115,
     117, 119, 120, 122, 131, 135, 144–145, *144*
Kruskall, Sarah, 26

Mahler, Gustav, 146, 151
Manfred Overture (Schumann), 129–130
Mendelssohn, Felix, 53
Merrill, Edys, 117–118, 119
Merritt, Arthur Tillman, 67
Mikado, The (Gilbert and Sullivan), 39–43
Minneapolis Symphony Orchestra, 73, 84, 146
Mitropoulos, Dimitri, 53–56, *55*, 73, 76, 80–81,
     84, 87, 96, 99, 100–102, 145–146, *145*
Montealegre, Felicia, 136
Moss, Phyllis, 90
Music for the Dance (Bernstein), 60, 150

New England Conservatory of Music, 11, 12, 26,
     117, 146
Newton, Massachusetts, 52, 54, 111, 148
New York Metropolitan Opera, 73
New York Philharmonic, 84, 120, 122, 125–133,
     134, 135–136, 146
"Now I Know" (Bernstein), 116

"Oh by Jingo," 3, 48
On the Town (Bernstein), 135, 140–141, 144, 151

Perry, Thomas "Tod," 104
Petrouchka (Stravinksy), 64
Piano Variations (Copland), 68, 70, 92
Pirates of Penzance, The (Gilbert and Sullivan), 60,
     143
Pittsburgh Symphony Orchestra, 81, 84, 119, 148
Porgy and Bess (Gershwin), 58
Porter, Cole, 49
Potash, Ruth, 44
Prairie, The (Foss), 142
Prall, David, 68
Prokofiev, Sergey, 145

Rachmaninoff, Sergey, 21
Ramin, Sid, 14–16, *15*, 18, 34, 46, 49, 52, 146–147,
     146
Ravel, Maurice, 20, 52, 64
Red Cross, 120–122
Reiner, Fritz, 81–84, *83*, 86, 87, 96, 102, 106, 119,
     122, 147–148, *147*
Respighi, Ottorino, 53
Revuers, 78, 116, 117, 140–141, 143–144
Rhapsody in Blue (Gershwin), 14, 52, 57
Rimsky-Korsakov, Nikolay, 81, 96
Robbins, Jerome, *79*, 144
Roberta (Kern), 49
Robinson, Mrs., 63–64
Rodeo (Copland), 142
Rodzinski, Artur, 120, 122–124, *123*, 127, 128
Room 57 (Shapero), 96
Rosenberg, Dorothy, 26
Roxbury, Massachusetts, 8, 9, 111
Rukeyser, Muriel, 68–70
Rumbalero (Gould), 27
Ryack, Eddie, 14–16
Rybernia, 16, 147

Samuel Bernstein Hair Company, 6, 11–13, 19, 36,
     37, 45, 72, 77, 111, 112–114, 116, 125, 133

Sandburg, Carl, 142

Scheherazade (Rimsky-Korsakov), 81, 96

Schnittken, Dana, 36

Schubert, Franz, 53

Schuman, William, 107–108

Schumann, Robert, 129

Serkin, Rudolf, 87, 88

Shapero, Harold, 67, 96, 148–149, *148*

Sharon, Massachusetts, 33, 34, 36–37, 39–44, 57, 62, 78, 100, 108, 111, 125

Sharon Community Players, 39–44, *44*

Shostakovich, Dmitry, 60, 115

Signet Society, 49–50

Singin' in the Rain (Comden and Green), 144

"Smoke Gets in Your Eyes," 49

Sokolow, Anna, 67, 68

Spiegel, Mildred, 25–27, *26*, 28, 34, 37, 39, 43, 53, 56, 60, 63–64, 67, 107, 150, *150*

State Symphony Orchestra, 64

Strauss, Richard, 130

Stravinsky, Igor, 64, 98

Stubbs, Hal, 49

"Sweet Georgia Brown," 48

Symphony Hall (Boston), 20, 21, 54, 96

Tanglewood, 94–102, *97, 98, 101,* 104, 106–108, *109, 110,* 115, 119, 120, 136, 143, 144, 145, 149

Temple Mishkan Tefila, 3, 19, 22

Thompson, Randall, 90, *91,* 102

Time Cycle (Foss), 142

Tin Pan Alley, 46–48, 57, 74, 116

Toscanini, Arturo, 27

Tourel, Jennie, 122, *126,* 127–128

Town Hall (NYC), 119, 127, 142

United Service Organizations (USO), 108, 112

Vengerova, Isabelle, 87–88, 89, 106

Verdi, Giuseppe, 24

Wagner, Richard, 73, 130

Walter, Bruno, xi, 127, 128, 129

West Side Story (Bernstein), 135, 143, 146–147, 151

"When the Moon Comes Over the Mountain," 16

William Lloyd Garrison School, 9–10

Williams, Susan, 11, 12, 27–28

Wonderful Town (Bernstein), 135

World War II, ix–x, 77, 78–80, 103, 108, 114, 115, 120

draft and, 103, 111–112, 120

"Yes, We Have No Bananas," 48

Young People's Concerts, 136, 148, 151

Zirato, Bruno, 125, 128, 129

Zvainboim, Sura-Rivka (aunt), 103–104